RANDOM KNOWLEDGE

Volume One

Bing Dingo

Copyright © 2024 Bing Dingo

All rights reserved

No part of this book may be reproduced, or stored in a retrieval system, or transmitted in any form or by any means, electronic, mechanical, photocopying, recording, or otherwise, without express written permission of the author.

Paperback ISBN: 9798336836059

Cover design by the author

Independently published

CONTENTS

Title Page
Copyright
Introduction
1: The Strange Lives of Deep-Sea Creatures   1
2: The Phenomenon of Déjà Vu   3
3: Forgotten Languages of the World   5
4: Peculiarities of Planetary Rings   7
5: The Secret Lives of Urban Animals   9
6: The Science of Coffee   11
7: Obscure Festivals from Around the Globe   13
8: Unusual Architectural Feats   15
9: The Curious History of Numbers   17
10: Quirky Animal Mating Rituals   19
11: The Enigmas of Easter Island   21
12: Unlikely Scientific Discoveries   23
13: Forgotten Inventions   25
14: The Peculiar World of Quantum Mechanics   27
15: Magical Realism in Literature   29
16: The Biodiversity of Rainforests   31
17: The Impact of Synesthesia on Perception   33
18: Optical Illusions and How They Work   35
19: The Culture of Politeness   37
20: The Mystery of Sleep Paralysis   39
21: The Theory of Spontaneous Generation   41

22: The Language of Whales	43
23: The Art of Bonsai	45
24: The Enigma of Dark Matter	47
25: Anomalous Weather Phenomena	49
26: The Intricacies of Moss	51
27: The Illusion of the Moon Landing Hoax	53
28: Techniques of Facial Reconstruction	55
29: The Puzzling World of Cryptography	57
30: Wacky World Records	59
31: The Psychology Behind Superstitions	61
32: The Mystery of Non-Newtonian Fluids	63
33: The Historical Impact of Salt	65
34: The Intricacies of Typographic Design	67
35: The Intriguing World of Synesthesia	69
36: The Science of Memory	71
37: The Mystique of Time Capsules	73
38: Bizarre Forms of Precipitation	75
39: The Mechanics of Cat Purring	77
40: The Physics of Soap Bubbles	79
41: The Secret Life of Words	81
42: The Peculiarities of Animal Behavior	83
43: The History of Odd Inventions	86
44: Eccentric Historical Figures	89
45: Strange Phenomena in Nature	91
46: Little-Known Scientific Facts	93
47: Unusual Cultural Practices	96
48: The Intricacies of Forgotten Technologies	99
49: Mysteries of the Human Body	101
50: Oddities in Art and Literature	103
51: Outlandish Legal Cases	105
52: The Wonders of Cryptids and Mythical Creatures	107
53: Quirky Architectural Marvels	109

54: The World of Uncommon Phobias	111
55: Anomalies in Space Exploration	113
56: The Culture of Conspiracy Theories	116
57: Unfamiliar Facts about Food and Drink	118
58: Uncommon Sporting Events	120
59: The Quirkiness of Timekeeping	122
60: Thoughts on Randomness	125
Afterword	129
Acknowledgement	131

INTRODUCTION

Welcome to *Random Knowledge Volume One* a curated exploration of the strange, the obscure, and the unexpected facets of the world around us. This book is for the curious mind that revels in discovering the hidden corners of knowledge that often go unnoticed in everyday life. Whether you find yourself fascinated by the deep mysteries of quantum mechanics, intrigued by the rituals of ancient festivals, or captivated by the odd behaviors of animals, this collection of random facts and stories offers a journey into the eclectic and the eccentric.

The idea for this book stemmed from a deep love for the bizarre and the overlooked—the facts that don't often make it into textbooks but are no less remarkable. The world is filled with hidden gems of information that defy conventional categories. From the unexplained phenomena of déjà vu to the enchanting practice of bonsai, each chapter takes you on a detour from the ordinary and invites you to question what you think you know about life, science, history, and beyond.

While each chapter stands alone, the topics are woven together by a common thread: the endless wonder that arises when we look closer at the overlooked details of our world. You might stumble upon the cultural impact of something as mundane as salt or be surprised by the intricacies of facial reconstruction techniques. These seemingly unrelated subjects are connected by the sheer joy of curiosity—a celebration of knowledge for knowledge's sake.

Whether you're flipping through these pages out of boredom, a thirst for trivia, or a desire to expand your intellectual horizons *Random Knowledge Volume One* offers something for everyone. The diversity of subjects is as vast as the unknown itself, and while the information contained within these pages may not change the world, it will hopefully inspire a sense of wonder and an appreciation for the quirky details that make life so fascinating.

So dive in. There's no need to read this book in order—feel free to skip around and explore whichever chapter catches your eye. In each section, you'll find a slice of knowledge that is peculiar, thought-provoking, and, above all, delightfully random.

Enjoy the journey.

1: THE STRANGE LIVES OF DEEP-SEA CREATURES

The deep-sea environment is one of the least explored and most mysterious habitats on Earth. This realm, characterized by crushing pressures, frigid temperatures, and complete darkness, harbors an array of life forms that appear more alien than terrestrial. Take, for instance, the giant isopods—creatures resembling oversized pill bugs that roam the ocean floor. These scavengers operate in the aphotic zone, where sunlight fails to penetrate, relying on whatever organic matter drifts down from above. Their ability to survive for long periods without food and their slow metabolism reflect a life of energy conservation and adaptation to scarcity.

Meanwhile, the anglerfish attracts attention with its grotesque yet mesmerizing appearance. Female anglerfish possess a bioluminescent lure that extends from their heads, a feature that emits light through a chemical reaction involving the enzyme luciferase. This adaptation is not merely for illumination but serves a predatory purpose—the light mimics the appearance of prey, drawing curious victims into the anglerfish's gaping maw. The disparity between the sexes in anglerfish is stark; males are diminutive and parasitic, fusing to the female's body and relying on her for nutrients.

Equally fascinating is the glass sponge, an organism that constructs its delicate lattice from silica. Despite its fragile appearance, the silica skeleton lends remarkable durability and resistance to the high-pressure environment. The intricate, vase-like structures of some glass sponges, such as the Venus' flower basket, provide a substrate for symbiotic shrimp that find refuge within. This biogenic silica formation is not only a marvel of natural architecture but also a testament to the complexity and interconnectedness of deep-sea life.

In contrast, the gulper eel showcases the bizarre adaptations necessary for survival in this forbidding habitat. Also known as the pelican eel, it exhibits an enormous mouth that can open wide enough to swallow prey much larger than itself. The lack of a rigid body structure allows the gulper eel to consume substantial quantities of food when the opportunity arises, a vital trait in a region where meals are sporadic and unpredictable.

Additionally, the elusive vampire squid straddles a liminal space between squids and octopuses, possessing characteristics of both. Luminescent arm tips and a cloak-like webbing between its limbs lend it an eerie, otherworldly appearance. Unlike its name suggests, the vampire squid feeds on marine detritus rather than blood, utilizing filamentous feeding appendages to gather organic debris that descends through the water column. These passive feeding mechanisms underscore the evolutionary pressures to exploit every possible niche in the nutrient-poor deep-sea environment.

Comprehending the entirety of deep-sea biodiversity involves more than just a catalog of strange bodies and behaviors. It demands an appreciation for the evolutionary ingenuity that enables life to flourish in settings that push physiological limits to their extremes. Consequently, these adaptations reveal not only the tenacity of life but also the intricate and often counterintuitive ways in which living organisms can thrive under the most inhospitable conditions.

2: THE PHENOMENON OF DÉJÀ VU

Déjà vu is an eerie sensation, a fleeting moment where one's surroundings feel uncannily familiar despite knowing they've never been encountered before. This phenomenon has puzzled scientists and laypeople alike, resting at the intersection of neurology, psychology, and even the fringes of the paranormal. Delving into the neurological basis behind déjà vu, we explore prominent theories and uncover how conditions such as temporal lobe epilepsy might trigger these disconcerting experiences.

The term "déjà vu" originated from the French, translating to "already seen." This term was popularized in the late 19th century by French scientist Émile Boirac. Although the sensation of déjà vu is nearly universal, affecting approximately two-thirds of the population at some point, its precise mechanisms remain elusive. Understanding déjà vu begins with examining how memory works within the human brain.

Memory can broadly be categorized into two types: declarative memory and non-declarative memory. Declarative memory refers to memories that can be consciously recalled, such as facts and events, while non-declarative memory involves skills and procedures, which operate without conscious awareness. Déjà vu appears related to the delicate interplay between these memory systems, particularly in regions of the brain like the medial temporal lobe, the hippocampus, and the parahippocampal gyrus.

One prominent theory posits that déjà vu arises from a "neural misfiring" in the medial temporal lobe, particularly the hippocampus, responsible for encoding and retrieving memories. In this theory, déjà vu occurs when there is a temporary glitch, causing the brain to erroneously signal that a new experience is familiar, despite evidence to the contrary. This misfire may prompt the sensation of recognition without the actual memory being present, creating the uncanny feeling of déjà vu.

Temporal lobe epilepsy (TLE) further elucidates this phenomenon. Individuals with TLE often report experiencing frequent déjà vu during seizures. These episodes of déjà vu are hypothesized to result from abnormal electrical activity specifically in the temporal lobe. This abnormality underscores the theory that disruptions in memory processing regions can produce the sensation of déjà vu, albeit in a more extreme and persistent form.

Another compelling theory is rooted in the concepts of dual-processing and temporal perception. This theory suggests that the brain processes sensory input through multiple pathways simultaneously. If one pathway experiences a slight delay, the information might reach conscious awareness twice in quick succession, creating the illusion that the second instance is a separate, familiar event. In essence, the brain perceives the repeated sensory input as a "memory" because of the microsecond lag between the pathways.

Some researchers also argue that déjà vu could be linked to the brain's method of checking memory integrity. This vetting process typically ensures experiences are cataloged correctly. Sometimes, however, this system might mismatches the new sensory input with stored memories due to overlapping similarities, triggering the sensation of familiarity. This theory aligns with the understanding that our memories are inherently reconstructive, constantly being updated, rather than entirely fixed recordings.

Interest in déjà vu extends beyond the realm of neurology and psychology, often finding its way into more esoteric discussions. Paranormal enthusiasts and some philosophers speculate that déjà vu could be related to past life experiences, parallel universes, or even precognitive abilities. While these interpretations lack empirical support, they highlight the deep cultural and existential significance attributed to the phenomenon.

Moreover, déjà vu has been subject to extensive research concerning its occurrence across different ages and demographics. Studies indicate that young adults, particularly those between the ages of 15 and 25, experience déjà vu most frequently. This observation might be attributed to the heightened neural plasticity and memory systems still evolving during these formative years. Additionally, factors such as stress, fatigue, and various perceptual complexities can influence the likelihood and frequency of déjà vu experiences.

Some investigations even touch upon the role of virtual reality and video games in inducing déjà vu. High-fidelity digital environments can mimic real-life experiences so closely that they might trigger the brain's familiarity sensors in a manner akin to traditional déjà vu. While not a perfect replica, these artificial experiences suggest the potential to study and perhaps even induce déjà vu under controlled conditions, offering future avenues for inquiry.

In summary, the phenomenon of déjà vu continues to intrigue and baffle, residing at the intriguing intersection of neuroscience, psychology, and cultural speculation. While significant strides have been made in understanding its possible neurological basis and triggering conditions, the sensation's fleeting and subjective nature ensures it remains a captivating enigma for both scientists and the general public alike.

3: FORGOTTEN LANGUAGES OF THE WORLD

Imagine peeling back the layers of time to encounter languages so ancient and enigmatic that their very essence eludes modern understanding. Languages like Linear A, Rongorongo, and Etruscan remain undeciphered, a mysterious vestige of forgotten eras. Linear A, originating from the Minoan civilization on Crete around 1800 to 1450 BCE, is inscribed on clay tablets and other artifacts. Its symbols give a glimpse into a sophisticated society, yet their meanings remain largely speculative. Linguists have devoted lifetimes attempting to decode these symbols, hoping to bridge the gap between the known and obscure.

Rongorongo, a system of glyphs found on Easter Island, tantalizes researchers with its potential insights into the island's societal structures and beliefs. Discovered on wooden tablets, often worn by weather and time, it remains one of the few undeciphered writing systems of the Americas. Unlike Linear A, where context and comparisons with later scripts offer some foothold, Rongorongo lacks a clear linguistic lineage, making interpretations even more speculative. Its potential linkage to the Polynesian maritime culture adds a layer of complexity, as differing theories about its origins abound.

The Etruscan language, spoken by the people of Etruria in ancient Italy, also defies full understanding. Though aspects of their script have been deciphered, allowing partial translations, the language itself lacks genetic relatives in the linguistic family tree. This isolation hampers comprehensive interpretation. Thousands of inscriptions, from monumental engravings to funerary texts, offer clues, but the full picture remains out of reach. Modern understanding of Etruscan life and culture is thus shaped more by archaeological artifacts than by written word.

The mystique surrounding these forgotten tongues captures the imagination, tantalizing linguists and historians alike as they struggle to unlock their secrets. As each undeciphered script surfaces, it comes with a promise—a promise of unlocking a narrative frozen in time. Understanding such languages is not merely an academic exercise but a quest to reclaim pieces of human history. Each symbol and glyph represents a voice from the past, eager to share its story yet speaking in riddles.

Digital technology and artificial intelligence offer new avenues for decipherment. By employing pattern recognition algorithms and massive linguistic databases, modern researchers hope to find linguistic parallels or recurrent structures within these ancient texts. These methods hold the promise of breakthroughs that were unimaginable for earlier scholars working manually.

The broader implications of deciphering these forgotten languages are profound. They could reveal trade routes, cultural exchanges, religious beliefs, and societal structures that have been lost to history. For cultures met with limited historical records, like the Minoans or the Rapa Nui of Easter Island, deciphering their languages would enrich our understanding immeasurably. It underscores the poignancy of lost knowledge and the fragility of cultural heritage.

Each glyph and symbol is a fragment of a bygone era, evoking both wonder and frustration. The process of decipherment is akin to piecing together a jigsaw puzzle without knowing what the final picture should look like. Every discovery, whether it's a tablet, a fragment, or even a single symbol, is celebrated for its potential to unlock new knowledge. Yet, the journey is fraught with false leads and dead ends.

The allure of forgotten languages lies not just in their ancient origins but in their promise of new narratives. In a world where information is instantaneously shared and languages evolve rapidly under the influence of globalization, these ancient scripts stand as silent sentinels of a time when human expression was nascent and diverse. They beckon us to look back even as we move forward, reminding us that understanding our past is a key to navigating our future.

4: PECULIARITIES OF PLANETARY RINGS

Saturn captures the imagination with its stunning rings, a feature so distinct that it often becomes the primary example when planetary rings are mentioned. Yet, it is not alone in this celestial adornment. Jupiter, Uranus, and Neptune, the other gas giants, also possess ring systems. These rings vary widely in size, composition, and visibility, each offering unique insights into their planets' histories and the processes that govern ring formation.

Saturn's rings are the most prominent and well-studied, stretching outward up to 282,000 kilometers from the planet. Composed predominantly of ice particles with trace amounts of rock debris, these rings are divided into seven major components labeled D to E, in order of their discovery. The particles range in size from tiny dust grains to chunks as large as houses. Cassini spacecraft's dives through the narrow gap between Saturn and its innermost ring revealed intricate, twisting structures within the material, attributed to the gravitational influences of Saturn's moons, such as Enceladus and Mimas. The source of these rings is a subject of ongoing debate, with theories suggesting they may be remnants of a destroyed moon or the result of cometary debris accumulation.

Jupiter's rings, discovered in 1979 by the Voyager 1 spacecraft, are much more subtle. They consist primarily of dust particles ejected from its moons' surfaces due to meteoroid impacts. The main ring, halo, and gossamer rings are faint and composed largely of microscopic debris, rendering them nearly invisible from Earth. Despite their faintness, these rings provide crucial information about the dynamic interactions between meteoroids and Jovian moons like Amalthea and Thebe.

Uranus presents a less flamboyant, yet equally intriguing ring system. Discovered in 1977 during a stellar occultation experiment, the rings of Uranus consist of 13 distinct components, mostly dark and narrow. The composition is thought to be primarily ice particles coated with a layer of dark, radiation-processed organic material. The planetary ring system's sharp edges belie ongoing interactions with Uranus's numerous moons. The rings are shepherded by these moons, whose gravitational influence helps maintain the rings' narrow and well-defined shapes.

Neptune's rings, identified during the Voyager 2 flyby in 1989, are even more mysterious. Composed predominantly of dust and ice particles, these rings exhibit clumpy, arc-like structures rather than uniform bands. The theory behind these arcs has piqued scientific curiosity—shepherd moons, gravitational resonances, or a combination of both, seem to mitigate the spread of ring material into arcs but the exact mechanism remains uncertain. While less dense and less bright compared to Saturn's, Neptune's rings shed light on the processes of ring confinement and stability in outer solar system conditions.

The formation and evolution of these rings involve complex, interwoven processes. Initial formation might stem from the disintegration of moons or cometary bodies under immense tidal forces near the planet. Over time, the gravitational influences of moonlets or shepherd moons shape and maintain the ring's structure. In Saturn's rings, the propeller-like formations—a result of interactions between small, embedded moonlets and the surrounding particulate matter—highlight localized disturbances and give astronomers insights into planetary moonlets' behaviors.

The interaction between rings and planetary magnetospheres also plays a significant role in shaping the rings' structures. Charged particles trapped in a planet's magnetosphere can influence ring particles, leading to changes in composition and visible features. For instance, Saturn's E-ring is influenced by the material ejected from the icy moon Enceladus's geysers, which interact with Saturn's magnetic field.

Understanding why only the gas giants have extensive ring systems poses a fascinating scientific challenge. Rocky planets like Earth and Mars might once have possessed rings, but proximity to the Sun and lack of significant moons to shepherd such features could have led to their rapid dissipation. Additionally, gas giants' extensive systems of moons and intense gravitational fields contribute to the stability and maintenance of their rings, a coupling absent or less pronounced in terrestrial planets.

Each ring system around the gas giants underscores the complexity and dynamism of planetary environments. They offer not only a visual spectacle but also a wealth of knowledge about planetary formation, moon-ring interactions, and the subtle forces shaping our solar system. The study of these rings continues to evolve, leveraging advancements in space exploration technology and observation techniques, gradually unveiling the intricacies of these celestial phenomena.

5: THE SECRET LIVES OF URBAN ANIMALS

Cityscapes teem with human activity, yet within this sprawling concrete, wildlife finds a niche, often unnoticed amidst the hustle and bustle. The raccoon, known scientifically as Procyon lotor, is a prime example of urban adaptability. These nocturnal creatures navigate through refuse bins and sewers, showcasing their dexterous paws and keen intelligence. In Toronto, for instance, raccoons have even figured out how to open green bins, designed to deter them. This minor engineering challenge only adds to their daily routine, blending seamlessly with their natural foraging behavior.

Foxes, especially the Red Fox (Vulpes vulpes), have also made cities their home. London boasts a significant population of urban foxes. These cunning animals have adopted an omnivorous diet, thriving on leftover food, small mammals, and even fruits from gardens. Urban foxes demonstrate altered behavior compared to their rural counterparts; they are less wary of humans and have smaller territories, suggesting a fascinating behavioral adaptation to dense human populations.

Pigeons, or rock doves (Columba livia), originally dwellers of sea cliffs, have found city buildings to be perfect substitutes. Their cooing is a familiar urban soundtrack. Pigeons have developed intricate social structures and homing abilities that baffle researchers. Studies reveal their navigation prowess, relying on a combination of magnetic fields, the sun, and even infrasound waves. Despite being often derogated as "rats with wings," these birds illustrate complex urban survival strategies.

Squirrels, particularly the Eastern Grey Squirrel (Sciurus carolinensis), commonly scurry through parks and suburban gardens. Their food caching behavior is both their survival tactic and a contributor to urban greenery, as forgotten nuts often sprout into trees. Squirrels are also known to create nests, called dreys, in the nooks of buildings, blending arboreal life with urban architecture. They exhibit remarkable problem-solving skills when accessing bird feeders or traversing obstacles.

The Norway rat (Rattus norvegicus), synonymous with urban environments, exemplifies resilience. These rodents can squeeze through gaps as small as half an inch, swim through sewer systems, and have a voracious reproductive rate. Their omnivorous diet and affinity for human refuse make them ubiquitous in cities worldwide. Beyond being pests, they are also subjects of scientific research due to their biological similarities to humans, contributing significantly to medical advancements.

Bats have adapted to roost in urban settings, often in attics or under bridges. Species such as the little brown bat (Myotis lucifugus) provide ecological services by consuming vast quantities of insects, including mosquitoes. Their echolocation skills enable them to navigate and hunt efficiently in dense urban environments, contributing to city ecosystems by controlling pest populations.

Honeybees (Apis mellifera) cohabitate in cities, with urban beekeeping gaining popularity. Rooftop apiaries exist in metropolises like New York and Paris. Urban bees often experience diverse nectar sources, potentially leading to rich and varied honey production. Interestingly, urban settings may sometimes expose bees to fewer pesticides compared to rural areas, offering a surprisingly conducive environment for their thriving.

In Australia, the Eastern Long-necked Turtle (Chelodina longicollis) has adjusted to urban waterways. These turtles navigate stormwater drains and man-made ponds, displaying the same slow, deliberate movements that have ensured their species' survival for millions of years. Their presence in urban environments serves as a reminder of nature's persistence amidst human alteration of landscapes.

Coyotes (Canis latrans) have become more common in North American cities, adapting their diets and hunting strategies. Sightings in Chicago, Los Angeles, and other urban areas highlight their expanding range. Coyotes utilize green corridors, such as railways and rivers, to move through cities, a testament to their opportunistic and adaptable nature. Their presence often spurs debates on wildlife management and coexistence in urban areas.

Feral cats (Felis catus) are ubiquitous urban dwellers. Their presence polarizes communities, prompting discussions on their impact on local wildlife and the importance of spaying and neutering programs. Despite living in the shadows, feral cats exhibit complex social behaviors and territoriality, similar to their domesticated counterparts. They are both predators and scavengers, contributing to their survival in diverse urban settings.

The European Starling (Sturnus vulgaris) thrives in cities with its iridescent plumage and mimicking calls. Introduced to North America in the 19th century, starlings have proliferated, demonstrating remarkable adaptability. They are known to exploit urban niches, nesting in cavities within buildings and feeding on a varied diet. Their presence in large flocks, or murmurations, is both a marvel and a nuisance in urban skies.

Thus, urban environments, while predominantly human-centric, host an intricate web of wildlife. Each of these species, with their unique adaptations and survival strategies, contributes to the rich tapestry of urban biodiversity. Understanding these animals' behaviors and interactions within city ecosystems not only broadens our appreciation of nature's resilience but also underscores the need for thoughtful coexistence practices in our increasingly urban world.

6: THE SCIENCE OF COFFEE

Every cup of coffee is an intricate dance of chemistry and physics, beginning long before the drink reaches the lips of millions each morning. Coffee's journey starts with the Maillard reaction during roasting, a chemical reaction between amino acids and reducing sugars that gives coffee its complex flavor profile, rich color, and enticing aroma. As the beans reach temperatures of around 370 to 540°F (188 to 282°C), they undergo numerous transformations, developing a spectrum of over 800 aromatic compounds.

The roasting process does not merely alter the beans' chemical composition; it drastically affects their physical properties. Beans expand in size, lose moisture, and their density changes. The roast profile—light, medium, or dark—impacts the solubility of compounds, ultimately influencing taste. Light roasts typically preserve more of the bean's original characteristics and acidity, while dark roasts enhance boldness and bitterness through prolonged caramelization.

Grinding is another critical step. Size matters because it determines the surface area exposed to water during brewing, which in turn influences extraction. A fine grind, such as that used for espresso, allows for a short, intense extraction period wherein hot water quickly permeates the grounds, capturing oils and soluble compounds. On the other hand, coarser grinds used for methods like French press involve a longer contact time, ensuring a full-bodied and rich brew.

Water quality and temperature also play pivotal roles. Optimal extraction occurs when water temperatures are between 195°F and 205°F (90.5°C to 96°C). Water that's too hot can over-extract bitter compounds, while water that's too cool may yield under-extracted coffee, lacking in complexity. Additionally, the mineral content of water—its hardness and softness—can enhance or hinder the brewing process. Minerals like magnesium and calcium contribute to the binding of flavor compounds, whereas highly purified water can produce a flat, uninspiring cup.

Caffeine, one of coffee's most prominent constituents, is a central nervous system stimulant that affects adenosine receptors in the brain, warding off drowsiness and promoting wakefulness. Each coffee varietal and preparation method results in varying caffeine content. For instance, a single espresso shot contains less caffeine than a typical serving of drip coffee due to its smaller volume, despite its stronger flavor.

The flavor profile of coffee is also influenced by its terroir—the combination of environmental factors where the coffee was grown. Altitude plays a significant role. Beans grown at higher elevations mature more slowly, developing denser and harder seeds that yield more complex flavor notes. Coffee from high-altitude regions, such as Ethiopia or Colombia, often features bright acidity and nuanced flavors. In contrast, beans grown at lower altitudes may develop a more straightforward, earthy taste.

Coffee's journey doesn't end with brewing. The same compounds that provide pleasure can deteriorate rapidly upon exposure to air, leading to oxidation and staling. Proper storage in airtight containers, away from light, heat, and moisture, can prolong coffee's flavor integrity. Freezing beans can also extend their shelf life without significantly impacting quality, a handy method for those who cherish their coffee supply.

Understanding the science of coffee elevates every sip from a simple pleasure to a profound appreciation of the underlying processes. It is a marriage of countless variables—temperature, pressure, time, and chemistry—all harmonizing to create the familiar beverage that invigorates both body and mind.

7: OBSCURE FESTIVALS FROM AROUND THE GLOBE

Festivals often serve as cultural touchstones, each reflecting the unique customs and values of its community. While globally recognized celebrations, such as Rio's Carnival or Munich's Oktoberfest, dominate headlines, equally fascinating yet lesser-known festivals thrive in the nooks and crannies of the world.

La Tomatina, held annually in the small Spanish town of Buñol, is the epitome of energetic chaos. It transforms the town into a war zone of ripe tomatoes. Participants, numbering in the tens of thousands, engage in a massive tomato fight, hurling overripe fruits at each other with gleeful abandon. The event begins with the "palo jabón," a greased pole with a ham atop it, and the frenzy only starts once someone manages to retrieve the prize. The origin of La Tomatina is unclear, but many speculate it began spontaneously in the mid-20th century, perhaps as a form of playful vandalism that stuck through the years. With its vivid red spectacle, La Tomatina leaves the town drenched but jubilant, a remarkable sight of human exuberance.

Halfway across the globe lies Japan's Obon festival, a solemn yet uplifting occasion that honors the spirits of deceased ancestors. Rooted in Buddhist traditions, Obon spans several days and encompasses various rituals, including the meticulous cleaning of graves and the offering of food to ancestral spirits. The most visually arresting component is the "Bon Odori," or Bon dance, performed by communities in circular formations, symbolizing the unity of the living with their departed loved ones. Floating lanterns, released onto rivers, lakes, and seas, guide spirits back to their resting place. The serene beauty of Obon juxtaposes La Tomatina's zany fervor, encapsulating a profound cultural reflection on life and death.

In the frozen expanse of the Netherlands, Elfstedentocht stands as a singular celebration of both endurance and camaraderie. Held irregularly due to its dependence on weather conditions, this ice-skating marathon covers approximately 200 kilometers, traversing through eleven historic Frisian cities. The event, first held in 1909, remains the ultimate test of a skater's skill and resilience. Participating in Elfstedentocht is a badge of honor, attracting tens of thousands when the ice is thick enough—an infrequency that only amplifies its allure. The camaraderie among participants and spectators, coupled with the stark beauty of the icy landscape, creates an unforgettable communal experience.

Traveling to South America reveals another unique event, the vibrant Inti Raymi in Peru. As a tribute to the Incan sun god Inti, this festival reaches back to pre-Columbian times but was reestablished in the 20th century. Held on June 24 in Cusco, the heart of the Inca Empire, Inti Raymi marks the winter solstice in the Southern Hemisphere—the Incan New Year. The central ceremony takes place at the Sacsayhuamán archaeological site, a sprawling complex of ancient walls and terraces. Elaborate reenactments of Incan rituals unfold, featuring participants clad in vivid traditional garments. The offerings to Pachamama, the earth mother, and Inti serve as poignant reminders of indigenous traditions adapted over centuries. Inti Raymi is a spectacle of history brought vividly to life, a tapestry of cultural heritage richly celebrated.

Meanwhile, in the isolated Norwegian village of Rjukan, the Rjukan Mirror Festival celebrates human ingenuity and adaptation. Deprived of direct sunlight for nearly half the year due to surrounding mountains, Rjukan installed massive mirrors in 2013 to reflect sunlight into the town square. The festival marks the beginning of "sun season," relishing the rare treat of natural light. Activities include outdoor gatherings, concerts, and communal sunbathing, all bathed in precious reflected sunlight. This modern celebration, rooted in technological innovation, underscores humanity's persistent quest to bend nature's challenges to its favor.

From obscure historical reenactments to technologically-altered festivities, the tapestry of global festivals paints a portrait of human diversity, creativity, and resilience. Each celebration, whether obscure or well-known, offers a lens through which one can observe the interplay of history, environment, and community. These festivals, spanning continents and cultures, provide more than mere entertainment—they are the heartbeat of cultural identity and continuity.

8: UNUSUAL ARCHITECTURAL FEATS

Gravity defies logic in the form of the Guggenheim Museum in Bilbao, Spain. Designed by Frank Gehry, this structure flaunts its unconventional curves and titanium cladding as a testament to the boundless potential of contemporary design. The museum appears to be an unfolding, metallic flower, drawing visitors not just for the art it houses, but for the art it represents. Gehry's use of cutting-edge design software allowed for unprecedented control over the form and flow of the building, showcasing how technology can expand the boundaries of human creativity.

In stark contrast to the modernity of the Guggenheim stands Petra, an ancient city carved directly into the rose-red cliffs of Jordan. This architectural marvel, crafted by the Nabataeans around 312 BCE, features structures like the Treasury and the Monastery. The precision with which these massive facades were chiseled from solid rock inspires awe, especially given the limited tools available at the time. Petra speaks volumes of the ingenuity and persistence of its creators, who transformed a desert landscape into an oasis of monumental architecture.

The feat of constructing the Sagrada Família in Barcelona, a project initiated by Antoni Gaudí, is another story of architectural ambition. Begun in 1882 and still under construction today, this basilica represents a fusion of Gothic and Art Nouveau styles. Gaudí's incorporation of organic forms, inspired by nature, and his structural innovations, such as the hyperboloid vaults, demonstrate his visionary approach to architecture. The towering spires, intricate facades, and vibrant stained glass are not just aesthetic elements but a reflection of Gaudí's deep-rooted beliefs and his desire to create a sacred space that resonates with spirituality.

On a completely different note, the Nakagin Capsule Tower in Tokyo, Japan, challenges traditional concepts of habitation. Designed by architect Kisho Kurokawa and completed in 1972, the tower consists of 140 prefabricated capsules stacked around a central core. These capsules, intended as micro-apartments or offices, can be individually removed and replaced, aligning with Kurokawa's vision of a metabolist city that evolves over time. The building's

LEGO-like modularity symbolizes adaptability and the fleeting nature of modern urban life.

Traveling back in time to the continent of Europe, the Leaning Tower of Pisa remains a symbol of architectural mishap turned triumph. Despite its unintended tilt, the tower, completed in 1372, continues to attract millions of visitors. Engineers and architects have spent centuries attempting to correct and stabilize its inclination, showcasing the continuous interplay between human ambition and the laws of physics. The Leaning Tower's preservation is a testament to our dedication to maintaining historical integrity while employing modern engineering solutions.

Meanwhile, the Lotus Temple in New Delhi, India, designed by Iranian-Canadian architect Fariborz Sahba, is a modern architectural feat that combines spirituality with form. Completed in 1986, this Bahá'í House of Worship features 27 free-standing marble-clad "petals" arranged in clusters to form a nine-sided flower. The architectural and structural complexity of the Lotus Temple mirrors the inclusive and unifying principles of the Bahá'í faith. Its symmetrical beauty and serene ambiance draw millions of visitors irrespective of their religious beliefs.

The Dubai Fountain, positioned at the base of the Burj Khalifa in the United Arab Emirates, embodies technological prowess in the realm of architecture. Designed by WET Design, the creators of the Bellagio Hotel Fountain in Las Vegas, this aquatic marvel spans over 900 feet and features jets that propel water up to 500 feet in the air. Choreographed to music and illuminated by lights, the Dubai Fountain encapsulates the fusion of art, technology, and spectacle. Its existence reinforces Dubai's commitment to pushing the envelope in urban and architectural development.

In yet another corner of the world, the Icehotel in Jukkasjärvi, Sweden, presents a continually evolving form of architecture. Reconstructed annually since 1989, using ice blocks from the nearby Torne River, this ephemeral structure serves as both a hotel and an art gallery. Each iteration of the Icehotel features unique designs, sculptures, and decor crafted by artists from around the world. The impermanence of the Icehotel challenges traditional notions of architecture, emphasizing experience over permanence and highlighting the delicate interplay between human creativity and natural materials.

Finally, the Great Mosque of Djenné in Mali, constructed in 1907, is a striking example of Sudano-Sahelian architecture. This massive structure, made entirely of sun-baked mud bricks (known as ferey), coated in a mud plaster, stands as the largest mud-brick building in the world. The mosque is renowned for its annual plastering festival, the Crepissage de la Grande Mosquée, where the local community comes together to apply a new coat of mud to protect and maintain the structure. This event underscores the relationship between architecture and communal identity, reflecting a deep cultural and environmental harmony.

9: THE CURIOUS HISTORY OF NUMBERS

Numbers are the invisible threads that stitch together the fabric of human understanding, transcending cultures and ages. Yet behind their seamless façades lies a history brimming with intrigue and complexity.

The concept of zero is one of the most significant inventions in mathematical history. The Babylonians used a placeholder for a missing number around 300 BCE, but it wasn't quite the zero we know today. It lacked the ability to function as a numeral in its own right. It was in ancient India, around 500 CE, that the mathematician Brahmagupta first formulated rules for zero's operation. He introduced zero as a number, alongside rules for arithmetic operations involving zero, such as subtracting a number from itself. Zero's adoption spurred new mathematical discoveries and eased the process of algorithmic computations, effectively reshaping mathematics and science.

Negative numbers, too, had a contentious journey into acceptance. Early mathematicians like the Greeks found the idea of less-than-nothing baffling. The Chinese, however, had already been using negative numbers in accounting records to denote debts as early as 300 BCE. The methodical Chinese arithmetic texts, "The Nine Chapters on the Mathematical Art," detailed rules for handling positive and negative numbers, yet European mathematicians would remain skeptical until at least the 16th and 17th centuries. During this period, figures like Gerolamo Cardano began to use negative numbers more regularly, albeit cautiously.

Irrational numbers further exemplify the complex tale of numerics. The discovery dates back to ancient Greece when Pythagoras' followers stumbled upon an unsettling fact while investigating the hypotenuse of a right triangle. The length, derived from the square root of two, couldn't be expressed as a ratio of two integers no matter how they tried. This revelation contradicted their belief that all numerical quantities were rational and reportedly caused significant internal disputes among the Pythagoreans.

Arabic scholars, specifically Al-Khwarizmi in the 9th century, played a crucial role in developing algebra (derived from the Arabic word "al-jabr"). His works translated into Latin introduced European scholars to Hindu-Arabic numerals and algebraic techniques, bringing a new era in mathematics. The symbol for "x" as the unknown variable in equations came much later, popularized by René Descartes in his 1637 work "La Géométrie."

Prime numbers intrigued and mystified mathematicians through the ages. The sieve of Eratosthenes, a systematic method of identifying primes, is a testament to the Greek mathematical prowess around 200 BCE. The distribution of primes reveals irregularities and patterns that form the basis of number theory, a field that fascinated Carl Friedrich Gauss in the 18th century and continues to be pivotal in modern cryptography.

Imaginary numbers began as mere figments of mathematical creativity, tasked with solving the otherwise unsolvable cubic equations. The Italian mathematician Rafael Bombelli, in the 16th century, was among the first to formalize the operations involving the square roots of negative numbers. It was, however, Leonhard Euler and Carl Friedrich Gauss in the 18th century who mainstreamed the usage of imaginary numbers, denoted as "i," the square root of -1. This conceptual leap paved the way for complex numbers, combining real and imaginary units, which now underpin much of quantum physics and electrical engineering.

Patterns within some numbers warranted entire careers of study. The Fibonacci sequence, derived from a rabbit-breeding problem introduced by Leonardo of Pisa in 1202, reveals a mathematical sequence where each number is the sum of the two preceding ones. Its significance extends beyond breeding models, reflecting natural patterns like the arrangements of leaves and the spirals of shells.

These various threads weave together a rich tapestry of numerical evolution, from zero's conceptual dawn to the present complexities of imaginary numbers and beyond. The journey reflects humanity's incessant quest to measure, understand, and manipulate the universe through the lens of mathematics. Through numbers, ancient mysteries dissolve, and new worlds of understanding continue to unfold.

10: QUIRKY ANIMAL MATING RITUALS

The natural world is rife with mating rituals that range from the peculiar to the downright bizarre. These behaviors are critical for species survival, yet they often defy human expectations of romance and courtship. Take, for instance, the bird of paradise, whose mating dance is as elaborate as it is captivating. The male bird performs a complex series of movements, including spreading its feathers into a fan, hopping about, and making various calls, all to entice a female. The brighter and more complex the display, the more likely the male will gain the female's favor.

Marine fireflies, on the other hand, utilize bioluminescence to attract mates. These small crustaceans emit light from specialized cells to create intricate patterns in the water. Males often gather in large groups, flashing in synchronized bursts to catch the attention of potential mates. The phenomenon is not just for show—it is a precisely timed event that requires a fine-tuned biological clock.

Some spider species have taken the concept of gift-giving to an entirely new level. Male nursery web spiders, for example, present females with a silk-wrapped parcel that often contains a nutritious insect meal. If the gift is deemed acceptable, the female allows the male to mate with her. Interestingly, some males attempt to deceive females by wrapping non-nutritive items such as leaves or bits of stone, although such deceit often doesn't yield successful mating.

In the world of seahorses, it is the males who undertake the responsibility of carrying and nurturing the offspring. During the mating ritual, males and females perform a courtship dance that involves spiraling around each other and changing colors. Once the dance concludes, the female deposits her eggs into the male's specialized pouch, where he fertilizes and incubates them until they hatch.

No discussion of quirky animal mating rituals would be complete without mentioning the bowerbird. Male bowerbirds are famous for constructing elaborate structures, called bowers, decorated with colorful objects like berries, flowers, and even plastic. The primary purpose of these bowers is to impress females. Each species of bowerbird has its own aesthetic preferences and building techniques, making it a fascinating example of nature's complexity in mating habits.

The praying mantis takes a more drastic approach to courtship. Females are known for their cannibalistic behavior, sometimes consuming the male during or after mating. This practice provides the female with a significant nutritional boost that can be crucial for egg production. While risky, the male mantis often adopts specific behaviors to minimize this risk, such as cautiously approaching the female and quickly retreating post-mating.

In the insect world, the dance fly showcases an intriguing mating behavior. Male dance flies present females with silk-wrapped prey, similar to nursery web spiders. However, in some species, males engage in deceit by presenting empty silk balloons. Females preferring larger prey have driven males to evolve this deceptive strategy to maximize their mating success.

Another mesmerizing example comes from the world of cuttlefish. These cephalopods are masters of disguise, capable of changing their skin color and texture in an instant. During mating season, male cuttlefish use their color-changing ability to dazzle females and ward off rival males. Smaller, less dominant males also adopt an alternative strategy by mimicking female coloration to sneak past larger males and gain access to potential mates.

The curious case of the Jacana, or "lily-trotter," turns conventional gender roles on their head. In this species, it is the female who is larger and more dominant, maintaining a territory with multiple males. The males, on the other hand, are responsible for incubating eggs and caring for the young. Female Jacanas often engage in aggressive battles to secure and maintain a harem of males, underscoring the diversity of mating systems even within the avian world.

Lastly, consider the courtship behavior of the blue-footed booby, a seabird renowned for its strikingly colored feet. Males perform an exaggerated high-stepping dance to showcase their vibrant blue feet to females. The brighter and bluer the feet, the more attractive the male is perceived to be, indicating good health and genetic fitness.

From the grand displays of birds of paradise to the deceptive gift-giving of spiders, the animal kingdom is a testament to the myriad ways species have evolved to reproduce. Each ritual, no matter how quirky or unconventional, plays a vital role in the perpetuation of the species, highlighting the incredible diversity and ingenuity of life on Earth.

11: THE ENIGMAS OF EASTER ISLAND

Easter Island, or Rapa Nui as it is known to its indigenous inhabitants, presents one of the most beguiling mysteries in human history. Situated in the southeastern Pacific Ocean, this remote island is best known for its Moai statues, which have captured the imaginations of archaeologists, historians, and the public alike. These monolithic human figures, carved from volcanic tuff, stand in silent rows and solitary positions across the rugged landscape. Their creation has given rise to numerous theories and debates regarding the engineering prowess and social organization of the Rapa Nui people.

The Moai, averaging 13 feet in height and weighing approximately 14 tons, are believed to have been carved between 1400 and 1650 CE. The exact methods employed in their transportation from quarry sites to their final locations are still a matter of conjecture. One popular hypothesis suggests the use of wooden sleds and log rollers, a technique that would have required significant manpower. Another theory posits that the statues were "walked" to their destinations by a sophisticated system of ropes and strategically applied leverage, an idea supported by modern experimental reconstructions.

Furthermore, the cultural and spiritual significance of these statues cannot be underestimated. The Moai are thought to represent deified ancestors, serving as guardians of the island's communities. Positioned on large stone platforms called ahu, these figures faced inland, overseeing the villages and the daily lives of the people. This configuration underscores the importance of ancestor worship and the belief in the protective power of the Moai.

The society responsible for these monumental undertakings experienced a dramatic transformation, leading to speculation about an environmental collapse. Deforestation, likely exacerbated by the overharvesting of the towering palms that once covered the island, led to soil erosion and decreased agricultural productivity. As resources dwindled, social cohesion deteriorated, culminating in tribal warfare and the toppling of many Moai statues. This narrative, while compelling, is contested by some scholars who argue for a more nuanced understanding of the island's ecological and societal changes.

Adding to the island's enigma is the Rongorongo script, a series of glyphs carved into wooden tablets and other objects. Despite significant efforts, this writing system remains undeciphered, providing tantalizing clues without yielding its secrets. If successfully deciphered, Rongorongo could offer invaluable insights into the history, beliefs, and daily life of the Rapa Nui people, potentially resolving some of the island's enduring mysteries.

Easter Island's isolation also played a significant role in shaping its unique culture. The nearest inhabited land is over 1,200 miles away, and contact with other Polynesian societies was minimal. This seclusion fostered a self-contained and distinctive civilization that developed in relative autonomy until European contact in the 18th century. The arrival of Europeans brought diseases, slavery, and other disruptions that further eroded the island's population and cultural heritage.

Today, Easter Island is a UNESCO World Heritage site, drawing visitors from around the globe. Efforts are ongoing to preserve the Moai and other archaeological treasures, as well as to revitalize the cultural practices and language of the Rapa Nui people. Current research continues to explore the interplay between human activity, environmental factors, and cultural evolution on the island, striving to piece together the complex narrative of this fascinating society.

Through these investigations, Easter Island remains a powerful testament to human ingenuity, resilience, and the enduring quest to understand our past. The statues stand as a mute but potent reminder of both the heights of achievement and the vulnerabilities that characterize human endeavor.

12: UNLIKELY SCIENTIFIC DISCOVERIES

Accidents and chance observations have often served as catalysts for major scientific discoveries, illustrating that the path to innovation is not always straightforward. One of the most renowned examples is the discovery of penicillin by Alexander Fleming in 1928. Fleming, a bacteriologist, had been studying the properties of the Staphylococcus bacteria. After returning from a two-week vacation, he noticed that a mold, later identified as Penicillium notatum, had contaminated one of his petri dishes. Remarkably, the area surrounding the mold was free of the bacteria. Fleming deduced that the mold secreted a substance capable of killing bacteria, which led to the development of penicillin, revolutionizing medicine and marking the advent of antibiotics.

In a similar vein, the invention of the microwave oven was a fortuitous byproduct of radar research during World War II. Percy Spencer, an engineer working for Raytheon, was testing a magnetron—a device used in radar systems—when he noticed that a candy bar in his pocket had melted. Intrigued, Spencer conducted additional experiments, eventually placing popcorn kernels near the magnetron, which promptly popped. Realizing the potential for a new cooking technology, Spencer and his team developed the first microwave oven, forever altering food preparation methods.

The discovery of synthetic dye also arose from unexpected circumstances. In 1856, William Perkin, an 18-year-old chemist, was attempting to synthesize quinine for malaria treatment. During one of his experiments, he noticed that a blackish residue turned a vibrant purple when diluted with alcohol. This accidental discovery of mauveine, the first aniline dye, catalyzed the birth of the synthetic dye industry, transforming fashion and textile manufacturing.

A closer inspection of these serendipitous discoveries reveals a common thread: an openness to anomalies and a willingness to explore the unexpected. When Charles Goodyear accidentally dropped a mixture of rubber and sulfur onto a hot stove in 1839, he wasn't initially aiming to create a durable material. The mixture charred but did not melt, and instead formed what we now know as vulcanized rubber. This new material demonstrated improved elasticity and resistance to heat, revolutionizing the rubber industry and leading to the production of tires, hoses, and an array of everyday products.

The world of scientific experimentation is replete with such instances where accidents and curiosity intersect. The pacemaker, an essential medical device, emerged from the failure of a less significant project. In 1956, engineer Wilson Greatbatch inadvertently inserted the wrong type of resistor into a prototype circuit, generating a pulsating electrical signal. Recognizing its potential, Greatbatch refined his creation, resulting in the development of the first implantable cardiac pacemaker, saving countless lives.

Another unintended yet vital discovery was X-rays by Wilhelm Röntgen in 1895. While experimenting with cathode rays, Röntgen noticed a glowing screen in his lab and realized that an unknown form of radiation was causing it. Named X-rays (with 'X' signifying the unknown), these rays could penetrate various materials, allowing for the imaging of bones and other internal structures. This discovery not only transformed medical diagnostics but also earned Röntgen the first Nobel Prize in Physics in 1901.

Even the sticky note owes its existence to a failed experiment. In 1968, Spencer Silver, a chemist at 3M, was trying to develop a super-strong adhesive. Instead, he produced a weak, pressure-sensitive adhesive that could be easily removed without leaving a residue. Initially at a loss for its application, Silver's invention found a purpose in 1974 when his colleague, Art Fry, used the adhesive to anchor bookmarks in his hymnal. This practical application led to the commercialization of Post-it Notes, a ubiquitous office product.

Observing how these diverse incidents led to groundbreaking advancements underscores the importance of adaptability and perceptiveness in scientific exploration. Discoveries like these highlight the unpredictable nature of research, where persistence and an inquisitive mindset can turn apparent failures into transformative innovations. Science often progresses not just through rigorous methodology but through unexpected insights that defy initial objectives, reminding us that sometimes, the most profound revelations occur in the most unplanned ways.

13: FORGOTTEN INVENTIONS

History is littered with inventions that failed to stand the test of time. Among these, the monowheel stands as a curious mixture of ambition and impracticality. Conceived as a single-wheeled vehicle, it featured a large outer wheel in which the rider sat and pedaled. The monowheel boasted an innovative design, attempting to combine the efficiency of a bicycle with the maneuverability of a unicycle. However, its inherent instability, limited speed, and the unsettling prospect of "gerbilling"—where the rider and inner frame could rotate freely within the outer wheel—rendered it a forgotten curiosity rather than a practical mode of transport.

The Dynasphere, another singular invention, followed a similar trajectory. Designed by Dr. J.A. Purves in the 1930s, this vehicle resembled a giant hoop, within which the driver sat. Propulsion came from an internal combustion engine or electric motors, depending on the model. Despite its futuristic appearance and imaginative engineering, the Dynasphere was hampered by its poor balance and difficulty navigating uneven terrains. Marketing it as the automobile of the future proved futile, as it struggled against the already well-established four-wheeled vehicles that populated the roads.

Equally intriguing is the invention of the baby cage, born out of a desire to provide urban infants with fresh air and sunlight. Originating in the early 20th century, these cages were designed to be attached to the exterior of apartment windows, creating a makeshift balcony for babies. The cages allowed infants to experience the outdoors while parents lacked the means or time to take them to parks. Although initially popular in crowded cities, safety concerns and evolving child-rearing practices led to the decline and eventual disappearance of the baby cage.

Blending a scientific approach with entertainment, the telectroscope captured imaginations in the late 19th century. Conceptualized by Alexander Graham Bell in 1878, this device promised to transmit visual images over long distances, akin to an early form of television. However, the technology of the time could not sustain Bell's ambitious vision, leaving the telectroscope as a fascinating footnote rather than a functional invention. It would take several decades for technology to catch up, eventually giving rise to modern television.

Another notable invention that failed to achieve widespread adoption is the jet pack. Popularized by science fiction and fervent inventors, the idea of personal aerial travel offered boundless excitement. In the 1960s, companies like Bell Aerosystems produced prototypes capable of short, controlled flights. However, concerns over safety, limited flight duration, and the sheer impracticality of individual jet packs for mass transportation relegated this promising invention to the realms of niche demonstrations and entertainment.

The world of forgotten inventions also includes everyday items like the 8-track tape, which, for a brief period, revolutionized the music industry. Introduced in the 1960s, 8-track tapes allowed listeners to enjoy continuous music playback without the interruption of flipping records. Their compact design made them suitable for car stereos, leading to widespread adoption. However, the emergence of cassette tapes, offering greater recording flexibility and smaller size, quickly overshadowed the 8-track, driving it into obsolescence.

Among medical inventions, the iron lung presents a poignant example of technological evolution. Developed in the 1920s and widely used during the polio epidemics, this negative pressure ventilator allowed patients with respiratory failure to breathe. Encasing the patient's body from the neck down, the iron lung mechanically regulated air pressure, mimicking the natural process of inhalation and exhalation. The advent of modern ventilators and the near-eradication of polio have largely replaced these cumbersome devices, but they remain emblematic of medical ingenuity and the human struggle against disease.

Another category of forgotten inventions pertains to failed communication devices. The pneumatic tube system, once a fixture in urban centers, served as an early concept of rapid transit for small packages and messages. Propelled through networks of tubes by compressed air or vacuum, these systems facilitated communication over short distances within buildings like hospitals and office complexes. Despite their efficacy, the rise of electronic communication and the impracticality of expanding these networks to larger scales rendered pneumatic tubes obsolete, though their legacy lives on in some sectors.

These forgotten inventions underscore the relentless march of progress, highlighting both the brilliance and the limitations of human creativity.

14: THE PECULIAR WORLD OF QUANTUM MECHANICS

Quantum mechanics is a branch of physics that fundamentally alters our perception of reality. It begins by discarding the deterministic approach of classical mechanics, introducing a probabilistic framework that seems counterintuitive. Superposition, entanglement, and the observer effect challenge our traditional concepts of how the universe operates.

One of the most perplexing aspects of quantum mechanics is superposition. This principle suggests that particles exist in multiple states simultaneously until observed. Schrödinger's cat paradox illuminates this concept by placing a cat in a hypothetical box with a poison that releases based on the state of a subatomic particle. Until the box is opened, the cat is simultaneously alive and dead. This thought experiment underscores the bizarre implications of quantum theory.

Entanglement goes a step further, revealing a form of connection between particles that defies spatial separation. When two particles become entangled, the state of one instantly influences the state of the other, regardless of distance. This phenomenon puzzled Einstein, who famously referred to it as "spooky action at a distance." Despite the unsettling implications, experiments continuously confirm the reality of entanglement, revealing a deeper layer of interconnectedness in the universe.

The double-slit experiment further defies classical intuition by demonstrating the dual nature of light and matter. When particles like electrons pass through two slits, an interference pattern emerges, indicative of wave behavior. However, when observed, particles revert to behaving like discrete particles, erasing the interference pattern. The act of measurement appears to collapse the wave function, a cornerstone of quantum interpretation that echoes through various philosophical debates.

Particle-wave duality extends to all quantum entities, not just photons or electrons. Louis de Broglie posited that particles possess wave-like properties, leading to the concept of matter waves. Quantum mechanics unifies this duality, showing that particles are neither purely waves nor particles but exhibit characteristics of both depending on the context of measurement.

Heisenberg's uncertainty principle introduces another layer of peculiarity, asserting that certain pairs of properties, like position and momentum, cannot be simultaneously known to arbitrary precision. The more accurately one property is measured, the less accurately the other can be determined. This intrinsic limitation is not a result of experimental error but a fundamental property of quantum systems.

Quantum tunneling adds to the strangeness, allowing particles to pass through potential barriers that classical mechanics deems impassable. This effect underpins many technologies, including the scanning tunneling microscope, which allows scientists to visualize surfaces at the atomic level. In the realm of stars, quantum tunneling is crucial for nuclear fusion, enabling particles to overcome repulsive forces that would otherwise prohibit fusion reactions.

The probabilistic nature of quantum mechanics is encapsulated in the wave function, a mathematical description of a quantum system's state. The interpretation of wave functions remains a topic of debate among physicists. The Copenhagen interpretation, spearheaded by Niels Bohr, posits that the wave function provides a complete description of a system's probabilities. Alternative interpretations, such as the Many-Worlds Interpretation, propose that all possible outcomes of quantum measurements do occur but in separate, branching universes.

In the realm of technology, quantum mechanics has paved the way for innovations like quantum computing. Quantum computers leverage superposition and entanglement to perform computations vastly more complex than classical counterparts. They have the potential to revolutionize fields such as cryptography, material science, and complex system modeling.

Ultimately, quantum mechanics invites us to reconsider our understanding of reality. It highlights the limitations of classical perspectives and opens vistas into the underlying fabrics of the universe. Each discovery in quantum mechanics not only answers questions but also poses new ones, maintaining an enduring sense of mystery and excitement in the quest to comprehend the nature of existence.

15: MAGICAL REALISM IN LITERATURE

Magical realism blends the mundane with the fantastical, creating worlds that feel familiar yet wondrous. This genre finds roots in Latin American literature, although it has since broadened its reach globally. Gabriel Garcia Marquez's "One Hundred Years of Solitude" serves as a quintessential example. The Buendía family's multigenerational saga unfolds in Macondo, a town where the extraordinary is commonplace. Remedios the Beauty ascends to heaven while hanging laundry, ghosts interact seamlessly with the living, and rain can last for years. Marquez's narrative presents these implausible events with a straightforwardness that renders them almost inevitable, a defining trait of magical realism.

Haruki Murakami, a contemporary Japanese author, infuses his stories with ordinary characters encountering surreal phenomena. In "Kafka on the Shore," a boy communicates with cats and a man can cause fish to rain from the sky. Despite these marvels, the characters react with calm acceptance, blurring the line between reality and fantasy. Murakami's works often reflect themes of loneliness and existential search, with magical elements enhancing rather than overshadowing the human experience.

Isabel Allende's "The House of the Spirits" blends family saga with elements of magic. Spirits visit family members, prophetic dreams come true, and characters exhibit supernatural abilities. Set against the backdrop of political upheaval in Chile, Allende's narrative weaves historical reality with mystical elements, creating a rich tapestry that explores themes of love, power, and destiny. The mystical occurrences serve to deepen the readers' connection to the characters, granting an otherworldly depth to their struggles and triumphs.

Jorge Luis Borges, another pillar of this genre, constructs labyrinthine stories where the metaphysical and fantastical come alive. In his collection "Labyrinths," constructs such as infinite libraries, books that can alter reality, and mirrors that can distort time challenge the boundaries of human perception. Borges's use of magical realism delves into the philosophical, prompting readers to question the nature of reality and the limits of human understanding.

In "Beloved" by Toni Morrison, the past manifests as a literal ghost that haunts the characters. Set after the American Civil War, the protagonist, Sethe, confronts the physical embodiment of her traumatic history. The spectral presence forces a reconciliation with past events, interweaving the personal with the supernatural.

Similarly, Salman Rushdie employs magical realism to critique social and political issues in "Midnight's Children." The protagonist, Saleem Sinai, is born at the exact moment of India's independence and possesses telepathic powers. Other characters born at the same moment have unique magical abilities, which allegorically represent the complexities and aspirations of a newly independent nation. Rushdie's narrative blends history with myth, the realistic with the supernatural, reflecting the multifaceted nature of India's cultural and political landscape.

Magical realism is distinguished from fantasy by its grounding in the real world. Authors present fantastical elements as just another part of everyday life. The tone remains matter-of-fact; characters do not question the fantastical occurrences, and neither do the narrators. This creates a seamless integration of the magical within the real, allowing readers to suspend disbelief without challenging the story's internal logic.

Alejo Carpentier coined the term "lo real maravilloso," or "the marvelous real," to describe the extraordinary aspects intrinsic to Latin American culture. This idea reflects in magical realism's portrayal of everyday life as infused with wonder. For instance, in Laura Esquivel's "Like Water for Chocolate," emotions directly influence physical reality. When Tita cooks, her feelings transform the food, causing anyone who eats it to mirror her emotional state. This heightened sense of reality, where emotions and the physical world intertwine, exemplifies the genre's core ethos.

In essence, magical realism invites readers to perceive the world through a lens where the impossible coexists with the ordinary. By merging the real with the magical, it challenges conventional distinctions between reality and imagination, encouraging a deeper exploration of human experience and perception.

16: THE BIODIVERSITY OF RAINFORESTS

Rainforests cover a minuscule portion of Earth's surface but harbor unparalleled biodiversity. Despite occupying less than 3% of the planet's total land surface, tropical rainforests are home to more than half of the world's plant and animal species. With towering canopies, thick understories, and pervasive moisture, these vibrant ecosystems are teeming with life, each layer bustling with an array of organisms adapted to unique niches.

In the canopy, the uppermost layer, sunlight is abundant, and this zone is dominated by tall, broad-leaved evergreen trees. Epiphytic plants, including orchids and bromeliads, thrive here, their roots suspended mid-air, absorbing moisture from the humid atmosphere. These plants exhibit a remarkable symbiosis with their arboreal hosts, often providing microhabitats for frogs, insects, and birds while extracting nutrients from decaying organic matter that accumulates on their host trees.

Descending to the understory, where sunlight is filtered through the dense overhead foliage, large leaves become a vital adaptation for plants to capture whatever light penetrates. Here, one finds a multitude of shrubs, ferns, and saplings vying for light and space. Many of these plants have developed ingenious methods to survive in the dappled light. For instance, some have evolved leaves that can adjust their orientation to optimize light capture, while others possess a darker green pigment to absorb more of the available spectral light.

The forest floor, the darkest part of the rainforest, presents an environment rich in decomposing matter, providing a fertile ground for fungi, microbes, and detritivores. Leaf litter, fallen branches, and decomposing fruits offer ample sustenance for creatures like earthworms, beetles, and millipedes, which play critical roles in nutrient cycling. Certain fungi in this layer form mutualistic relationships with tree roots, enhancing nutrient uptake for both partners—a crucial interaction in such nutrient-poor soils.

Among the arthropods, rainforest ants and termites are ecological engineers, constructing elaborate nests and decomposing vast quantities of organic material. Leafcutter ants, notable for their complex social structures, forge symbiotic relationships with fungi cultivated in their underground nests. Termites, similarly, break down dead plant material, facilitating nutrient recycling that supports new plant growth.

Rainforests are also the realms of unique and specialized vertebrates. Birds such as toucans and parrots, with their vivid plumage and resonant calls, inhabit the middle and upper canopies. Their diets of fruits, nuts, and seeds contribute significantly to seed dispersal, aiding in forest regeneration. In contrast, ground-dwelling species like peccaries and tapirs act as ecosystem gardeners, trampling vegetation and dispersing seeds through their waste.

Amphibians, particularly frogs, exhibit remarkable biodiversity in rainforests. Poison dart frogs, with their aposematic coloration, warn predators of their toxicity. Their varied reproductive strategies, ranging from laying eggs on leaves to carrying tadpoles to water-filled bromeliads, highlight their adaptability. Meanwhile, reptiles such as the green iguana or the well-camouflaged chameleon epitomize the evolutionary innovations necessary to thrive in such dynamic environments.

Rainforest mammals, while often elusive, constitute an important part of these ecosystems. Primates, such as spider monkeys and orangutans, possess advanced locomotive and cognitive abilities to navigate the arboreal maze and forage for seasonal fruits. The jaguar, an apex predator, maintains the balance by controlling populations of herbivores, illustrating the intricacies of the food web.

In addition to the well-known creatures, millions of insects, many of which remain undiscovered, contribute to the rainforest's complexity. These insects participate in pollination, predation, and decomposition, each fulfilling an essential ecological role. The interdependence among plants, insects, and other animals reinforces the idea that rainforests are finely tuned ecosystems, where the removal or decline of a single species can have cascading effects throughout the biome.

The unique climatic conditions of rainforests also contribute to their ecological complexity. High humidity and consistent warm temperatures support continuous plant growth, resulting in a year-round supply of food for herbivores and the predators that follow. The seasonal patterns, shaped more by precipitation than temperature, influence flowering and fruiting cycles, leading to periods of abundance and scarcity.

Human activities, however, pose significant threats to rainforest biodiversity. Deforestation for agriculture, logging, and infrastructure development leads to habitat fragmentation and species decline. Conservation efforts, including the establishment of protected areas and sustainable management practices, are crucial in preserving these irreplaceable ecosystems.

Rainforests, with their extraordinary biodiversity, exemplify the delicate balance of nature. Understanding and appreciating the complexity of these ecosystems is vital for their conservation and the well-being of countless species, including our own.

17: THE IMPACT OF SYNESTHESIA ON PERCEPTION

Synesthesia is a neurological phenomenon where stimulation of one sensory pathway leads to automatic, involuntary experiences in a second sensory pathway. This condition manifests in various forms, with the most common types being grapheme-color synesthesia, where letters or numbers are perceived as inherently colored, and chromesthesia, where sounds elicit visual colors and shapes. Although synesthesia affects a small portion of the population, it offers unique insights into human perception and cognition.

One classic example is when a person with grapheme-color synesthesia perceives the letter "A" as inherently red, while the letter "B" might be blue. This form of synesthesia can profoundly impact everyday experiences, from reading a book to interpreting numerical data. The consistency of color associations for specific graphemes suggests that synesthesia is a stable trait, likely rooted in neural connections established during early development.

Scientists believe that synesthesia results from cross-wiring or increased connectivity between adjacent sensory areas in the brain. For example, in grapheme-color synesthesia, the area of the brain responsible for processing letters and numbers is situated near the region involved in color perception. Functional magnetic resonance imaging (fMRI) studies have shown that when synesthetes perceive graphemes, their color-processing regions are activated even in the absence of actual colored stimuli.

Chromesthesia, or sound-color synesthesia, involves the perception of colors when hearing sounds, including music, speech, or environmental noise. A person with chromesthesia may see specific hues or dynamic color patterns while listening to a symphony or even during a casual conversation. This form of synesthesia can enhance musical experiences, as synesthetic musicians often report that their condition aids in memory and composition. Famous musicians like Franz Liszt and Duke Ellington exhibited signs of chromesthesia, describing their experiences in vivid detail.

The linkage between auditory and visual perception in chromesthesia hints at broader questions about the integration of sensory information in the brain. While non-synesthetes perceive sound and color through distinct, unconnected pathways, synesthetes experience a merging or fusion of these sensory modalities. This suggests that the brain's sensory processing regions maintain a level of plasticity that allows for such atypical connections.

Beyond grapheme-color and chromesthesia, synesthesia can take on numerous other forms, such as lexical-gustatory synesthesia, where words trigger taste sensations, or spatial-sequence synesthesia, where sequences like numbers, days of the week, or months of the year are perceived spatially in specific locations. Each form provides a different window into the complexities of sensory perception and neural architecture.

Lexical-gustatory synesthesia is particularly intriguing because it involves a link between language and taste. For instance, a person might find that the word "Thursday" tastes like chocolate or the name "John" evokes the flavor of strawberries. This condition affects not just the perception of spoken words but also written and internally thought language. Understanding lexical-gustatory synesthesia sheds light on the role of language in sensory integration and the potential for cross-modal associations in the human brain.

Spatial-sequence synesthesia, another captivating type, involves a visual and spatial component where sequences are perceived along specific spatial frameworks. Someone with this form of synesthesia might visualize the months of the year arranged in a circle surrounding their body or see numbers ascending in a three-dimensional space. The experiences of spatial-sequence synesthetes highlight the brain's ability to map abstract concepts, like time and numbers, onto physical space, revealing a spatial organizational framework within cognitive processes.

In recent years, research has turned towards understanding the genetic and developmental aspects of synesthesia. Studies with identical and fraternal twins indicate a strong genetic component, suggesting that synesthesia runs in families. However, the exact genetic mechanisms remain elusive, likely involving multiple genes and complex interactions between them. Environmental factors during critical periods of brain development might also play a role in shaping synesthetic connections, emphasizing the interplay between innate and experiential aspects of this condition.

Synesthesia's implications extend beyond individual sensory experiences, informing broader discussions on perception, creativity, and neural plasticity. Synesthetic experiences challenge traditional views of sensory boundaries and demonstrate the brain's remarkable capacity for creating perceptual experiences that integrate multiple modalities. By studying synesthesia, scientists can gain deeper insights into the neural basis of sensory processing, the nature of subjective experiences, and the extraordinary variability of human cognition.

18: OPTICAL ILLUSIONS AND HOW THEY WORK

Optical illusions intrigue the human mind by presenting visual puzzles that challenge our perception of reality. These illusions arise through various mechanisms, often exploiting the ways in which the brain interprets visual information to create misleading or deceptive images.

One common type of optical illusion is the geometric illusion. A well-known example is the Müller-Lyer illusion, where two lines of equal length appear different due to the orientation of arrow-like ends on each line. The brain's interpretation of the line's context prompts this misperception, demonstrating how surrounding visual cues can influence our perception of size and length.

Another captivating category is physiological illusions, which result from excessive stimulation of certain visual pathways. A classic instance is the Hermann grid illusion, where dark blobs seemingly appear at the intersections of a white grid on a black background. This occurs because of the way our retinal cells respond to light and dark contrasts, leading to a temporary but pervasive false perception.

Cognitive illusions, meanwhile, arise from subconscious inferences made by the brain. The Kanizsa triangle exemplifies this phenomenon, where an arrangement of Pac-Man-like figures creates the impression of a white triangle that does not exist. This illusion highlights how the brain tends to perceive complete shapes even when only partial information is available, showcasing its proclivity for pattern recognition and closure.

The Ames room illusion distorts spatial perceptions through a cleverly constructed room that appears normal when viewed from a specific viewpoint but is actually trapezoidal in shape. Objects and people within the room appear to change size dramatically as they move, exploiting the brain's assumption that rooms are typically rectangular and that parallel lines should converge at a vanishing point.

Ambiguous images present another form of visual trickery, where a single image can be interpreted in multiple ways. The famed Rubin vase illusion is a straightforward example; it can be seen either as a vase or as two faces in profile, with the brain able to switch between the two interpretations but not grasp both simultaneously. This shifting perception underscores the brain's flexibility and its role in constructing coherent visual experiences.

Optical illusions also encompass motion illusions, which deceive the sense of movement and can be particularly mesmerizing. The rotating snakes illusion, composed of static concentric circles, appears to exhibit continuous motion under certain conditions. This effect is achieved through contrasting colors and patterns that simulate the appearance of motion by fooling the motion-detecting cells in the visual cortex.

The study of optical illusions offers insights into the workings of the human visual system and the brain's interpretative processes. Scientists utilize these illusions to probe how vision works, how brain perception processes visual signals, and the intrinsic limitations of our perceptual apparatus.

Surrealist artists like M.C. Escher famously exploited optical illusions in their works. Escher's "Relativity" constructs an impossible world where gravity functions differently for various figures in the scene. Such artistic explorations demonstrate the interplay between art, perception, and cognitive processes, revealing how profoundly our understanding of the visual world can be shaped and manipulated.

Optical illusions are not just novelties; they serve practical purposes in both scientific and artistic contexts. Their ability to reveal the underlying principles of visual perception continues to provide valuable insights, challenging our assumptions and expanding our knowledge of how we interpret the world around us.

19: THE CULTURE OF POLITENESS

Politeness is often considered a universal virtue, yet its expression varies dramatically across different cultures. In Japan, for instance, bowing demonstrates respect and can signify various things depending on its depth and duration. The custom of bowing has been so ingrained in Japanese culture that it extends beyond person-to-person interactions into digital correspondences and company logos, where angled lines evoke a bowing gesture.

Meanwhile, in many Western countries, politeness tends to revolve around verbal expressions such as "please," "thank you," and "excuse me." These small phrases act as lubricants for social interactions, easing the potential friction between individuals. However, the importance of these expressions can differ even within the West. For instance, Nordic countries like Sweden and Denmark often favor a straightforward, low-context style of communication where excessive politeness might be perceived as unnecessary or insincere.

In contrast, in cultures where collectivism and hierarchical social structures are pronounced, such as in many parts of Asia and Africa, politeness involves a series of intricate behaviors and rules. Honorifics in language, differential seating arrangements, and even the specific way one passes objects can all carry significant weight. In South Korea, for instance, age and social status heavily influence how individuals address one another and the types of gestures they employ. The youngest in the group often pour drinks and serve elders as a sign of respect.

Moving over to South America, in Brazil, personal space during conversations tends to be smaller than what one might find comfortable in a country like the United States. Touching and close proximity signify warmth and friendliness. As such, backing away or avoiding contact could be construed as rudeness. Hospitality also plays a crucial role; refusing offered food or drink multiple times may be necessary before it is considered polite to accept.

In Russia, formalities matter a great deal, especially upon first meetings. A firm handshake alongside direct eye contact often sets a respectful tone. When invited to a Russian household, it's customary to bring a gift, often something symbolic like flowers, albeit in odd numbers—since even numbers are reserved for funerals.

Africa presents another fascinating venue for the study of politeness. In many African cultures, the community holds primacy over the individual, and greetings extend beyond a mere "hello" to questions about one's health, family, and even livestock. For instance, in parts of Nigeria, a greeting can turn into a small conversation, demonstrating genuine concern and respect for the person greeted. Interrupting such interactions might be seen as impolite and disrespectful.

In Middle Eastern cultures, hospitality takes on almost sacred dimensions. Guests are considered gifts, and their comfort is paramount. Offering tea or coffee repeatedly is a common practice, and accepting these offers is essential. Furthermore, polite conduct often includes the avoidance of the left hand for eating or passing items, as it's traditionally associated with less savory activities.

Politeness norms can also shift with time, technology, and globalization. Digital etiquette is becoming significant, bridging the gap between face-to-face politeness and online interactions. Emojis, punctuation, and even the timing of messages can convey politeness—or the lack thereof—just as powerfully as spoken words.

In sum, the culture of politeness is a fascinating mosaic of behaviors, traditions, and customs. Understanding these nuances not only makes social interactions smoother but also offers deep insights into the cultural fabric of societies around the world.

20: THE MYSTERY OF SLEEP PARALYSIS

Sleep paralysis is a phenomenon that leaves individuals temporarily unable to move or speak while falling asleep or upon waking. It is often accompanied by vivid hallucinations and a sense of suffocation, which can be profoundly unsettling. Despite having a basis in our physiology, the experience has long been enshrouded in mystery and has influenced folklore and cultural interpretations worldwide.

Physiologically, sleep paralysis occurs during the transition between wakefulness and REM (Rapid Eye Movement) sleep. During REM sleep, our most vivid dreams unfold, and our brains temporarily paralyze our major muscle groups to prevent us from acting out these dreams. Sleep paralysis happens when this mechanism persists as a person wakes up or falls asleep, resulting in the unsettling state where one is mentally awake but still physically in the depths of REM atonia.

Various factors contribute to the likelihood of experiencing sleep paralysis, including sleep deprivation, irregular sleep schedules, and certain sleep disorders like narcolepsy. Stress and sleeping on the back are also commonly associated with this phenomenon. Genetic predisposition might play a part, although it is less well understood. Statistics indicate that approximately 8% of the general population has encountered sleep paralysis at least once in their lifetimes, with higher occurrences reported among students and individuals with psychiatric conditions.

Hallucinations during sleep paralysis typically fall into three categories: intruder hallucinations, incubus hallucinations, and vestibular-motor hallucinations. Intruder hallucinations involve the perception of a threatening presence in the room, often shadowy figures or ill-defined entities. Incubus hallucinations are characterized by a sensation of pressure on the chest, sometimes interpreted as an assault by a supernatural being. Vestibular-motor hallucinations encompass out-of-body experiences and sensations of floating or flying.

Culturally, sleep paralysis has been interpreted in myriad ways. In Japanese folklore, it is referred to as "kanashibari," implying a feeling of immobility induced by a vengeful spirit.

Scandinavian cultures have tales of the "Mare," a malevolent creature that sits on the chests of sleepers, giving rise to the word "nightmare." In some African communities, the phenomenon is attributed to witchcraft or demonic visitation. These cultural attributions underscore the universal yet deeply personal nature of sleep paralysis encounters.

Scientific interest in sleep paralysis is relatively recent. Historical accounts provide documentation dating back hundreds of years, but systematic studies began in earnest in the late 20th century. Researchers utilize polysomnography and self-reporting through sleep diaries to gather data, aiming to understand the underlying neurological and psychological mechanisms. The phenomenon is often studied within the broader context of parasomnias, which also include sleepwalking and night terrors.

Effective management of sleep paralysis largely relies on improving sleep hygiene and addressing underlying conditions. Maintaining a consistent sleep schedule, avoiding sleep deprivation, and creating a comfortable sleep environment can reduce the frequency of episodes. Cognitive-behavioral therapy targets the anxiety often associated with sleep paralysis, helping individuals reshape their reactions and diminish the distressing impact of their experiences.

Despite advances in understanding, the precise neurological pathways involved in sleep paralysis remain elusive. Some theories propose that the brain's motor cortex is momentarily decoupled from the brainstem's arousal systems, leading to a mismatch between consciousness and the ability to move. Another hypothesis posits that REM sleep intrudes into wakefulness, causing dreamlike hallucinations to merge with reality.

The study of sleep paralysis bridges neuroscience, psychology, and cultural studies, offering insights into the complex interplay between brain activity and subjective experience. It serves as a potent reminder of how deeply our physiological states influence our perception of reality, blending the borders of the tangible and the ethereal in the fleeting moments between sleep and wakefulness.

21: THE THEORY OF SPONTANEOUS GENERATION

Spontaneous generation is an outdated biological theory that proposed life could arise from non-living matter without the need for reproduction from existing organisms. For centuries, this idea dominated scientific thinking. Aristotle, one of its early proponents, suggested that life forms such as fleas could emerge from inanimate substances like dust. The theory persisted because of observable phenomena that seemed to support it, like maggots appearing on decaying meat or mice in rotting hay.

The theory received considerable support from various observations. For instance, in environments lacking clear biological origins, such as stagnant water or decomposing organic matter, life seemed to manifest spontaneously. The appearance of maggots in meat, mold on bread, and even frogs in muddy soil bolstered the belief that life could emerge in a spontaneous and unconstrained manner.

Scientific inquiry in the 17th century started to cast doubts on the validity of spontaneous generation. One of the critical figures who challenged this theory was Francesco Redi, an Italian physician. Redi conducted experiments showing that when meat was protected from flies, no maggots appeared, thus linking the appearance of maggots to fly eggs being laid on the meat rather than spontaneous genesis. His work dealt a significant blow to spontaneous generation, although it did not entirely dismantle the theory.

Further experimentation by Lazzaro Spallanzani in the 18th century added more evidence against spontaneous generation. By boiling nutrient broths and sealing them in containers, he demonstrated that the broths remained free of microbial life unless exposed to air, suggesting that microorganisms did not spontaneously generate but came from the environment.

The definitive refutation of spontaneous generation came with the experiments of Louis Pasteur in the 19th century. Pasteur designed a series of experiments using swan-neck flasks that allowed air to enter but prevented microbial spores from reaching the broth inside. The clear results showed that no microbial life developed in the broth unless it was exposed to direct microbial contamination, conclusively demonstrating that life does not arise spontaneously.

While Pasteur's experiments were instrumental in debunking spontaneous generation, they also provided a foundation for the development of germ theory, which posits that many diseases are caused by microorganisms. This shift in understanding paved the way for advances in microbiology, immunology, and medicine.

Despite its eventual disproval, the theory of spontaneous generation represented a significant stage in the history of scientific thought. It illustrated how scientific ideas could persist over centuries despite conflicting evidence and highlighted the importance of rigorous experimentation in challenging established beliefs.

The demise of spontaneous generation transformed our understanding of life and its origins. It underscores a fundamental principle in biology: life arises from pre-existing life, a concept crystallized in the Latin phrase "Omne vivum ex vivo."

22: THE LANGUAGE OF WHALES

The ocean, an expansive and largely uncharted frontier, houses some of the most intelligent and enigmatic creatures known to humanity: whales. For centuries, these majestic marine mammals have fascinated scientists and storytellers alike, largely due to their sophisticated forms of communication. Whales don't just make random noises; they produce a complex series of clicks, whistles, and songs that form a genuine language, one we've only just begun to understand.

The first significant revelation about whale communication surfaced in the 1950s, when researchers realized that humpback whales produce long, intricate songs. These songs, typically sung by males during the breeding season, can last for hours and are often repeated with precision. Unlike human songs that can be relatively static, humpback whale songs evolve over time, with new themes phased in while others fall out of favor in a gradual process that's somewhat analogous to cultural shifts in human music.

Beluga whales, often referred to as "the canaries of the sea," present another fascinating case. Their range of vocalizations includes high-pitched whistles, clicks, and even what can be described as mews or chirps. Belugas are highly social animals, and their sounds are thought to serve a range of functions from locating prey through echolocation to maintaining social bonds within their pods. Their complex repertoire is suggestive of a rich, multifaceted communicative system.

Sperm whales are also notable for their unique sounds, which mainly consist of clicks. These clicks are not random but instead form rhythmic sequences known as "codas." Different pods of sperm whales exhibit distinct coda patterns, implying a form of dialect or clan-specific language. Furthermore, individual whales have unique clicks, akin to a personal identifier, which suggests sophisticated social structures and individual recognition.

The technology to study these vocalizations has become increasingly sophisticated. Hydrophones, underwater microphones capable of capturing a wide range of frequencies, allow researchers to record and analyze whale sounds with outstanding clarity. These recordings are often visualized using spectrograms, graphical representations that depict the frequency, duration, and intensity of the sounds, thus enabling detailed analyses of their structure and variations.

In recent years, the application of machine learning and artificial intelligence has accelerated our understanding of whale communication. By feeding vast datasets of whale vocalizations into learning algorithms, scientists can begin to decipher patterns and even predict behaviors. For instance, certain sounds are correlated with feeding, while others might indicate social interactions or navigational cues.

Despite these technological advancements, the true depth of whale language remains elusive. Most scientists agree that whale vocalizations likely serve multiple purposes, blending echolocation, communication, and even possibly a form of emotional expression. There are parallels to human language, such as syntax and context-specific variations, but the full scope of meaning behind these whale sounds is far from fully decoded.

The physical mechanisms that whales use to produce these sounds are equally fascinating. Baleen whales such as humpbacks generate sounds via their larynx, albeit without vocal cords. The exact mechanics remain a bit of a mystery, as observing these processes in a living whale is technically challenging. Toothed whales, like orcas and dolphins, use a specialized structure called the "phonic lips" located in their nasal region. These structures allow them to produce a wide range of sounds with remarkable control.

Orcas, or killer whales, provide another layer of complexity. They are known to possess distinct cultural groups, often referred to as ecotypes, each with unique vocal traditions. Resident orcas, which primarily hunt fish, have a different vocal repertoire compared to transient orcas, which hunt marine mammals. These vocal distinctions are so pronounced that they can be used to identify the orca's ecotype, much like recognizing regional accents in human speech.

In essence, the study of whale language is not merely academic; it has profound implications for conservation. Understanding these vocalizations can assist in monitoring whale populations, enforcing marine protected areas, and mitigating the impacts of human activities such as shipping and naval exercises. Noise pollution, for instance, poses a significant threat, as increased underwater noise from human sources can drown out whale communications and disrupt essential behaviors like mating and feeding.

The language of whales embodies an ancient and intricate form of communication, reflecting not just their interactions with each other but also their relationship with the vast oceanic environment. As technology and methodologies advance, the enigmatic songs, clicks, and whistles of these ocean giants might one day be fully understood, offering deeper insights into one of the most captivating phenomena in the animal kingdom.

23: THE ART OF BONSAI

The art of bonsai is a horticultural practice that transforms the growth of trees into miniature, aesthetically pleasing forms. Originating from the Chinese practice of penjing, it was eventually refined and popularized by the Japanese. The term "bonsai" literally translates to "planted in a container," encapsulating the essence of the tradition: crafting small trees that reflect the beauty and scale of their larger counterparts.

Bonsai is not merely about keeping a tree small but involves a series of techniques that require precision, patience, and artistry. Pruning is a fundamental aspect, where branches and roots are meticulously cut to maintain the desired shape and size. The method of wiring, using either copper or aluminum wires, allows branches to be bent and guided into specific directions, creating a balanced and harmonious form. These wires are left on until the branches set in their new positions, a process that can take several months.

The selection of species is crucial in bonsai. Certain trees naturally adapt to the constraints of a container, such as the Japanese maple, juniper, and pine. Each species has its unique requirements regarding light, water, and temperature. The grower must be attuned to these needs, ensuring that the plant remains healthy despite its confined environment.

The containers used in bonsai are as important as the plants themselves. Ideally, they should complement the tree, enhancing its visual appeal without overshadowing it. These pots come in various shapes, sizes, and colors, each chosen to accentuate specific features of the bonsai. For example, a round pot might be used for a tree with a cascading form, while an angular pot might suit a strong, upright tree.

Soil composition is another critical component. Bonsai soil must offer excellent drainage while retaining enough moisture to nourish the tree. Typically, a mixture of akadama, pumice, and lava rock is used, proportions varying depending on the tree species. This balance ensures the roots have access to oxygen, preventing root rot—a common issue in overly wet soils.

Watering is an art in itself. Bonsai trees can quickly dry out due to their reduced soil volume and the shallow nature of their pots. The frequency of watering depends on several factors, including the tree species, pot size, soil type, and environmental conditions. A skilled bonsai artist can tell by the feel of the soil or the weight of the pot whether the tree needs water.

Seasonal care is essential for maintaining the health and appearance of the bonsai. During the growing season, typically spring and summer, more frequent pruning and shaping are necessary as the tree is more vigorous. In autumn, the focus shifts to reinforcing the tree's structure and health, while winter often requires protective measures against severe cold, depending on the species and climate.

Repotting is a process undertaken every few years to replenish the soil and provide space for root growth. The tree is carefully removed from its pot, old soil is brushed away, and roots are pruned to encourage fine root development. This process rejuvenates the tree, promoting a healthy and balanced structure.

The aesthetic principles of bonsai are deeply influenced by Zen Buddhism, emphasizing simplicity, balance, and natural beauty. A well-crafted bonsai should evoke a sense of age and endurance, often through techniques like jin and shari, which involve creating deadwood features to mimic the natural aging process of trees subjected to harsh elements. This practice adds a dramatic, weathered appearance, heightening the bonsai's overall character.

Bonsai exhibitions and competitions are common, where enthusiasts showcase their meticulously cultivated trees. These events are opportunities for artists to display their skill and for the public to appreciate the subtle complexity and beauty of bonsai. These gatherings foster community and exchange of techniques, bolstering the continued evolution of the art.

Cultural significance imbues bonsai with more than aesthetic value; it symbolizes harmony, tranquility, and the delicate balance between nature and human effort. For many, bonsai cultivation is a meditative practice, demanding mindfulness and a deep connection with the living organism. This bond between creator and creation transforms bonsai into more than just horticulture; it becomes a lifelong pursuit of beauty and serenity.

The art of bonsai, with its rich history and intricate techniques, continues to captivate and challenge those who engage with it. It is a timeless tradition that encapsulates the essence of nature, shaped by human hands into living masterpieces that inspire contemplation and admiration.

24: THE ENIGMA OF DARK MATTER

The universe, vast and expansive, holds a profound mystery in the form of dark matter. Unlike the transparent clarity of stars and galaxies, dark matter remains shrouded in an almost primordial obscurity. It neither emits nor absorbs light, rendering it invisible to traditional telescopic methods. Yet its presence is undeniably felt through gravitational effects on visible matter. Galaxies, for instance, spin faster than their observable mass should permit, hinting at an unseen force bolstering their rotational speed.

Early indications of dark matter arose from the observations of Fritz Zwicky in the 1930s. Noticing that the Coma Cluster's galaxies moved at perplexing velocities, he posited the existence of "missing mass." This speculation was met with skepticism until subsequent spiral galaxy rotation curves, meticulously mapped by Vera Rubin and Kent Ford in the 1970s, corroborated his claims. Stars at the galactic periphery, Rubin observed, orbited at speeds inconsistent with the visible matter alone, further solidifying the dark matter hypothesis.

The composition of dark matter has eluded definitive identification. Prevailing theories suggest it could be comprised of WIMPs (Weakly Interacting Massive Particles). These hypothetical particles, if existent, interact predominantly through gravity and only weakly via other forces, making them arduous to detect. Experiments such as the Large Underground Xenon (LUX) and XENON1T have endeavored to capture direct interactions of WIMPs with ordinary matter, yet results remain inconclusive.

Alternately, axions, another candidate, propose an extremely light and feebly interacting particle that might constitute dark matter. Experimental setups like the Axion Dark Matter Experiment (ADMX) attempt to detect axions converting into photons in the presence of strong magnetic fields. Despite significant advances, axions remain hypothetical, a tantalizing possibility within the realms of quantum chromodynamics (QCD).

Gravitational lensing presents a compelling indirect method to study dark matter. Massive objects, dark matter inclusive, warp spacetime, bending light from distant sources and producing observable distortions. By scrutinizing these lensing effects, astronomers infer the mass and distribution of dark matter. The Bullet Cluster exemplifies this phenomena, where interacting galaxy clusters reveal a separation between visible matter and the dark matter inferred from gravitational lensing.

Anomalies in the cosmic microwave background (CMB) further suggest dark matter's omnipresence. The CMB, a relic radiation from the Big Bang, exhibits minute temperature fluctuations. These subtle variations provide a cosmic map, encoding the universe's early conditions. Data from the Planck satellite indicates that dark matter constitutes approximately 27% of the universe's total energy density, dwarfing ordinary matter's paltry 5%.

Despite compelling evidence, alternative hypotheses challenge the dark matter paradigm. Modified Newtonian Dynamics (MOND) proposes altering gravitational laws at cosmic scales to account for observed discrepancies without invoking unseen matter. While MOND explains certain galactic rotational anomalies, it struggles with clusters of galaxies and the intricacies of the CMB, leaving dark matter as the more robust explanation.

Dark matter's elusive nature propels ongoing research and experimentation. Particle accelerators like the Large Hadron Collider (LHC) search for signs of dark matter through high-energy collisions, hoping to glimpse heretofore unseen particles. Should WIMPs or other candidates be produced under controlled conditions, it would illuminate pathways toward understanding this cosmic enigma.

As astrophysics delves deeper into dark matter, interdisciplinary approaches merge observational astronomy, particle physics, and cosmology. Collaborative efforts and cutting-edge technology continue to chisel away at the darkness. While definitive identification remains on the horizon, the quest for dark matter epitomizes humanity's unyielding pursuit of the unknown, unraveling the universe's most profound secrets, one particle at a time.

25: ANOMALOUS WEATHER PHENOMENA

Weather phenomena have long fascinated and baffled humankind, prompting myths, stories, and scientific inquiry. Certain weather events defy conventional explanations and continue to intrigue meteorologists and laypeople alike. Among these is the phenomenon of ball lightning, an inexplicable occurrence where luminous, spherical objects appear during thunderstorms. The mechanics of ball lightning remain obscure, with theories ranging from electrically charged plasma to micro-black holes, yet no definitive explanation has been universally accepted.

In another corner of anomalous weather, rains of animals—such as frogs, fish, and even spiders—have been documented worldwide. These occurrences often involve tornadic waterspouts or strong wind currents lifting creatures into the atmosphere, only to release them miles away. The auditory element of weather is another source of wonder. Skyquakes, loud booming sounds from the atmosphere, are reported globally, yet their origin remains elusive. Some attribute them to natural phenomena like escaping methane hydrates or seismic activity, while others point towards man-made causes. Nevertheless, they are a reminder of the atmospheric mysteries that still evade scientific scrutiny.

The phenomenon of fire whirls, essentially tornadoes that form in conjunction with wildfires, further complicates our understanding of weather impacts. These fire whirls can spin at high velocities, causing devastating damage and spreading flames across wider areas. The conditions that create them—specific wind patterns, heat sources, and terrain configurations—illustrate the complex interplay between atmospheric dynamics and terrestrial phenomena.

Similarly perplexing are frost flowers, delicate ice formations that appear on the surface of young sea ice or plants in cold, calm conditions. They form as water vapor expelled from ice or plant surfaces encounters freezing air, creating intricate structures that resemble blooming flowers. The precise conditions under which they form and the beauty they exhibit pose intriguing questions for climatologists and casual observers alike.

Lenticular clouds, those lens-shaped formations often mistaken for UFOs, are another atmospheric puzzle. Their formation is linked to the flow of air over mountain ranges, creating standing waves in the atmosphere. When moisture in the air condenses at the crest of these waves, lenticular clouds materialize, stationary and often in stacks. Their smooth, saucer-like appearance enhances their mystique, feeding into cultural lore and skepticism.

A less visually enchanting but equally curious phenomenon is that of colored rain, sometimes referred to as "blood rain" when tinged red. Microscopic particles such as desert sand, volcanic ash, or pollen carried aloft can tint raindrops as they descend. This natural spectacle, documented throughout history, fueled superstitions and awe. Modern science provides clarity on the particulate causes, yet their unpredictability retains a sense of wonder.

Then there are halos, light phenomena produced by the refraction and reflection of sunlight or moonlight through ice crystals suspended in the atmosphere. These halos, which include rings, arcs, and spots of light around the Sun or Moon, come in various forms such as sun dogs and the 22-degree halo. The optical intricacies and conditions necessary to form these halos elicit both scientific interest and artistic inspiration.

On the subject of cold phenomena, the occurrence of ice storms, where freezing rain coats surfaces in a layer of ice, offers another layer of complexity. These storm conditions require a precise alignment of temperature gradients extending through layers of the atmosphere, with above-freezing air atop a sub-freezing surface layer. The aftermath can be both beautiful and catastrophic, as trees, power lines, and infrastructure succumb to the weight of the ice.

The transient yet dramatic events known as microbursts exemplify other atmospheric anomalies. These small-scale downdrafts that spread upon hitting the ground can cause extensive damage, mimicking the effects of tornadoes. The study of microbursts, particularly their genesis within thunderstorms and their short-lived yet potent nature, continues to advance our understanding of severe weather phenomena.

Thus, anomalous weather phenomena present a plethora of natural events that blur the line between scientific explanation and the marvel of unpredictability. These phenomena collectively highlight the vast, often unfathomable complexities inherent in the Earth's atmospheric system, inviting continued exploration and awe.

26: THE INTRICACIES OF MOSS

Moss, those small, dense clumps of green that often line forest floors and damp surfaces, forms an underappreciated cornerstone of terrestrial ecosystems. Comprised of tiny, non-vascular plants, mosses belong to the division Bryophyta, and their simplicity belies a remarkable ability to adapt and thrive in diverse environments.

The life cycle of moss is dominated by the gametophyte stage, a stark contrast to the vascular plants where the sporophyte stage is predominant. In mosses, the gametophyte is the green, photosynthetic structure most people recognize. It engages in producing gametes: sperm and eggs. These gametes unite in water, a necessity due to the sperm's flagella which require a film of moisture to swim to the egg. This process often renders mosses highly dependent on humid conditions for reproduction.

Once fertilization takes place, the sporophyte grows directly from the gametophyte, a remarkable symbiotic relationship where one stage of life depends entirely on the other. The sporophyte consists of a stalk (seta) topped with a capsule (sporangium). Within the capsule, spores are produced through meiosis and, once mature, are dispersed by the wind to germinate into new gametophytes under suitable conditions.

Mosses are pioneers in colonization, often the first to establish themselves on bare soil, rocks, or disturbed areas. Their simple structure enables them to anchor themselves in places where other plants cannot. Their ability to absorb water and nutrients directly through their leaves allows them to thrive on nutrient-poor substrates. This, paired with their capacity to retain moisture, makes them invaluable in preventing soil erosion and providing a damp, micro-climatic environment for other plant species to germinate.

An interesting adaptation of mosses is their resistance to desiccation. Many species can dry out completely and become dormant, only to revive and resume normal metabolic functions once water becomes available again. This property allows mosses to withstand environments characterized by periodic droughts, such as rock surfaces exposed to the elements.

Mosses also contribute significantly to the ecology by forming a critical part of the forest floor, providing habitat and sustenance for a multitude of small organisms. In boreal forests, Sphagnum moss is particularly notable for its role in forming peat bogs. Sphagnum mosses can hold vast amounts of water, contributing to the acidity and nutrient-poor conditions that characterize peat bog ecosystems. Over millennia, the accumulation of dead Sphagnum creates peat, which not only acts as a carbon sink but also serves as historical archives of past climatic conditions.

The importance of mosses extends beyond their immediate ecological function. Mosses have been utilized by human societies in various ways. Historically, peat moss has been used as a fuel source due to its high carbon content. Indigenous peoples have employed sphagnum moss for its absorbent properties, using it as a natural antiseptic dressing for wounds. Today, mosses are of interest in biotechnology fields for their potential in bioindication, surveying environmental health, and their impressive ability to bioremediate contaminated sites by absorbing heavy metals and other pollutants.

Their aesthetic and functional versatility also finds modern application in horticulture and landscaping, especially in creating lush, green living walls and Japanese-style gardens. Terrariums employing moss create self-sustaining ecosystems, and bonsai enthusiasts often utilize moss to add an aged look to their miniature trees.

Consequently, despite their diminutive size and simplicity, mosses wield a significant ecological influence. Their role in pioneering habitats, combating erosion, supporting biodiversity, and impacting the atmosphere's carbon balance, all denote their vital place in the natural world. The intricate, often unnoticed life of moss reveals a sophisticated interplay of biology and environment, a testament to the complexity and ingenuity inherent in even the smallest forms of life.

27: THE ILLUSION OF THE MOON LANDING HOAX

In 1969, NASA's Apollo 11 mission successfully landed the first humans, Neil Armstrong and Edwin "Buzz" Aldrin, on the Moon while Michael Collins orbited above in the command module. Yet, this extraordinary event, hailed as a monumental achievement in human exploration, is not without its detractors. A significant number of people remain convinced that the Moon landing was a hoax, meticulously staged on Earth. Their claims fall under various categories, relying heavily on perceived inconsistencies in photographic evidence, physical phenomena, and geopolitical context. To understand this conspiracy theory, one must comb through both the purported anomalies and the scientific explanations that rebut them.

Central to the conspiracy is the assertion that the photographs and videos from the Moon missions contain anomalies that cannot be explained if they were genuinely taken on the lunar surface. Skeptics often point to shadows in these images, claiming they appear to fall in directions inconsistent with a single light source—the Sun. They argue this could only be achieved with multiple lighting angles typical of a studio set. However, experts explain that the uneven lunar terrain can cause shadows to fall in various directions. Additionally, the reflective properties of the lunar surface scatter sunlight, causing the seemingly odd shadow patterns.

Another focal point of the conspiracy revolves around the American flag planted on the Moon, which appears to wave in several images and videos. Skeptics argue that in the vacuum of space, where no atmosphere exists to induce movement, the flag should remain entirely still. However, the flag actually contains a horizontal rod to keep it extended, giving the illusion of ripples or a waving motion. When astronauts planted the flagpole into the lunar soil, their actions likely caused the flag to move, and this movement persisted due to the lack of atmospheric drag on the Moon to dampen it quickly.

Further suspicions arose from the apparent absence of stars in the sky in the lunar surface photographs. Conspiracy theorists argue that these images should show a backdrop littered with stars, as seen from an atmosphere-free environment. The counter-argument posits that the camera settings used by the astronauts, which were designed to capture the bright lunar landscape and the astronauts themselves, had exposure times too short to capture the relatively faint light of distant stars. This phenomenon is akin to why stars often fail to appear in photographs taken on Earth at dusk or dawn.

Questions have also been raised about the radiation belts surrounding Earth, known as the Van Allen belts. Conspiracy theorists suggest that these belts contain lethal levels of radiation, rendering any passage through them by unshielded astronauts impossible. However, while the Van Allen belts do indeed contain radiation, the Apollo missions were well-planned for limited exposure time, minimizing risk through quick transit. Further, the spacecraft provided sufficient shielding, and the astronauts wore dosimeters to monitor radiation levels, which remained within safe limits for the duration of the mission.

Geopolitical context plays a significant role in the Moon landing hoax theories. The era of the Space Race was deeply embedded in Cold War tensions between the United States and the Soviet Union. Skeptics argue that the Moon landing served as a powerful propaganda tool to demonstrate technological supremacy over the Soviet Union. They believe that the United States would have done anything, including staging a fake landing, to assert its dominance. However, this overlooks the extent of the public and international scrutiny the missions endured. The Soviet Union, possessing its sophisticated space tracking capabilities, would have likely debunked any falsified claims, yet they acknowledged the American achievements.

Technical and operational details of the landing itself have also come under scrutiny. Conspiracy theorists question the feasibility of the landing procedure, specifically the intricate process of descent, landing, and subsequent ascent from the lunar surface. They doubt the capabilities of the computational technology available at that time, often citing the relatively primitive onboard computers compared to modern standards. Yet, the mission's success was a product of rigorous calculations, extensive simulations, and expertise in manned spaceflight operations developed over successive missions in the Gemini and Apollo programs.

Finally, samples of Moon rocks brought back by various Apollo missions serve as empirical evidence. These samples undergo analysis by diverse scientific communities worldwide, and their mineral composition differs markedly from Earth rocks, particularly in their lack of water content and unique isotopic signatures. Conspiracy theorists dismiss these differences as fabricated, yet the consistency across various international studies and the broader scientific consensus point to the Moon origin of these samples.

The Moon landing hoax remains one of the most enduring conspiracy theories in modern times. However, the evidence supporting the authenticity of the lunar landings is comprehensive and multifaceted, encompassing photographic analysis, radiation measurements, geopolitical rationales, and scientific sampling. While the claims of skeptics continue to circulate, they struggle to find footing against the robust body of evidence affirming humanity's remarkable achievement in space exploration.

28: TECHNIQUES OF FACIAL RECONSTRUCTION

Facial reconstruction employs techniques that span both art and science, blending forensic anthropology and anatomical knowledge to recreate human faces from skeletal remains. The primary objective is to produce a likeness that may aid in identifying unidentified remains, either in archaeological contexts or modern forensic cases.

Practitioners start with a detailed examination of the skull, noting key features such as the size and shape of the nasal aperture, the contour of the chin, and the overall cranial structure. These characteristics provide vital clues about the individual's age, sex, and ancestry. Measurements are meticulously taken, providing the framework for the reconstruction process.

The next step often involves adding tissue-depth markers to the skull. These markers, which vary based on demographic data, indicate the average thickness of soft tissues at various anatomical points. References like the Gerasimov method or American tissue depth charts guide this step, ensuring a degree of consistency in reconstructions.

Clay is often the medium of choice for the initial build-up of facial musculature. This approach allows for a tactile exploration of the underlying structures. Muscle groups are sculpted layer by layer, starting with the deepest groups and progressing to the surface muscles. Commonly, experts replicate muscles like the temporalis, masseter, and orbicularis oculi, which significantly influence facial contours.

Forensic artists then move on to skin and surface features. The application of clay shifts to sculpting the nose, lips, and ears—each feature shaped not just by soft tissue depth but also the interpretive expertise of the artist. The construction of the nose uses nasal spine and aperture dimensions to infer its prominence and shape, while the mouth is aligned with dental records and jaw structure.

Another vital aspect is hair. The skull provides limited clues about hairstyle, often based only on cultural and contextual clues, if any are available. Eyebrow shape, eyelash length, and other details are integrated based on probabilities and artistic judgment rather than definitive evidence.

Color is added next, especially in techniques extending to three-dimensional digital models. Digital reconstructions rely on CT scans or photogrammetry to recreate the skull in a virtual environment. Software applications then allow for a highly detailed, manipulable model that can be shared and refined collaboratively. The addition of color involves skin tone approximations based on population datasets and aging factors.

Specialists also incorporate radiographic superimposition, where skeletal remains are compared with photographs of potential matches. This non-invasive method overlays skull x-rays with life photographs, contrasting anatomical landmarks like the orbital cavities and zygomatic arches.

Facial reconstructions are not without limitations. The subjective aspects of reconstruction mean that variations occur between different practitioners, and certain soft tissue features like wrinkles, blemishes, and scars remain beyond exact replication. Public reception and the usefulness of images can vary, relying heavily on the frame of reference of both the forensic artist and investigators.

Despite these challenges, the amalgamation of anthropological rigor and artistic ingenuity in facial reconstruction remains a powerful intersection of disciplines. Each reconstructed face serves as a tangible bridge between the past and present, merging art's interpretative depth with science's empirical backbone.

29: THE PUZZLING WORLD OF CRYPTOGRAPHY

Cryptography, the art and science of encoding and decoding messages, has long been a cornerstone of secret communication. Its history stretches back to ancient civilizations. Early examples include the use of hieroglyphics in Egypt and the more technologically advanced encryption methods employed by the Greeks, such as the Scytale. The Romans took a profound step with the Caeser Cipher, a method of shifting letters within the alphabet that allowed important commands and communications to remain confidential.

During the Middle Ages, the complexity of cryptographic methods increased substantially. The polyalphabetic cipher, pioneered by the Italian scholar Leon Battista Alberti, introduced a system using multiple cipher alphabets, rendering frequency analysis —a method of breaking ciphers by examining the rate at which certain letters appear— ineffective. This period also saw the emergence of steganography, where hidden messages are concealed within seemingly innocuous texts or images.

The dawn of the 20th century revolutionized cryptography. Machines such as the Enigma, employed by the Germans during World War II, brought cryptographic complexity to new heights. The Enigma's reliance on electrical rotors and plugboard settings created numerous cipher permutations. This made it exceptionally challenging to decipher without knowledge of the specific daily settings. However, the collaborative efforts of cryptanalysts, including Alan Turing and his team at Bletchley Park, ultimately succeeded in breaking the Enigma code, substantially altering the course of the war.

With the advent of the digital age, the focus shifted towards computer-based cryptography. The introduction of the Data Encryption Standard (DES) in the 1970s established a new benchmark for data protection, although it was eventually superseded by the more robust Advanced Encryption Standard (AES) due to concerns over its security. Public-key cryptography, introduced by Whitfield Diffie and Martin Hellman, marked another revolution. Unlike traditional symmetric-key systems where the same key is used to encode and decode messages, public-key cryptography involves a public key for encrypting and a private key for decrypting, ensuring a higher degree of security and facilitating safe online transactions.

Quantum cryptography, a frontier yet to be fully realized, promises unbreakable encryption based on the principles of quantum mechanics. Quantum key distribution (QKD) employs quantum particles such as photons to create a shared secret key. Any attempt to intercept or measure these particles inevitably alters their state, alerting the communicating parties to the presence of an eavesdropper. While still in its infancy and constrained by practical technological challenges, quantum cryptography may redefine secure communications in the near future.

Cryptography has become indispensable in daily life. Virtually every digital transaction—from online banking to private messaging—relies on complex cryptographic algorithms for security. Protocols such as Secure Sockets Layer (SSL) and Transport Layer Security (TLS) ensure that data transmitted over the internet remains private and intact. Blockchain technology, which underpins cryptocurrencies like Bitcoin, utilizes cryptographic hashing to secure and verify transaction records, further demonstrating the integral role of cryptography in modern innovations.

30: WACKY WORLD RECORDS

From the longest fingernails to the highest number of hot dogs eaten in ten minutes, world records capture human attempts to push boundaries. They often verge on the bizarre, capturing attention and inspiring both awe and bewilderment. One such record is held by Lee Redmond, who started growing her nails in 1979. Her fingernails reached a combined length of 28 feet 4.5 inches before she tragically lost them in a car accident in 2009. Another peculiar record involves the most t-shirts worn at once, achieved by Sanath Bandara of Sri Lanka, who wore 257 t-shirts, one over the other, creating a veritable fabric fortress around him.

Competitive eating has its fair share of astonishing records. Takeru Kobayashi, a Japanese competitive eater, made a mark by consuming 110 hot dogs in 10 minutes during the 2010 Nathan's Hot Dog Eating Contest. Joey Chestnut holds the current record, having devoured 75 hot dogs and buns in the same time span in 2020. The speed and capacity with which competitive eaters can consume food often raise questions about both their physical and mental preparation, involving extensive training regimes and unique techniques to stretch their stomach capacity.

In the realm of artistic endeavors, Garry Turner of Britain set a record for the stretchiest skin. Turner, who has a rare medical condition called Ehlers-Danlos Syndrome, demonstrated the extent of his skin's elasticity by stretching the skin on his stomach to a length of 6.25 inches. Another impressive record involves the longest time spent in direct, full-body contact with ice, set by Wim Hof, also known as "The Iceman." Hof immersed himself in ice for 1 hour, 52 minutes, and 42 seconds, utilizing his unique breathing technique and mental training to withstand the extreme cold.

Animals also partake in the world of records. The fastest tortoise, a natively slow creature, surprises many with its speed records. Bertie the tortoise ran 0.92 feet per second, setting a new benchmark for his species. Cats, too, feature in records; the record for the loudest purr by a domestic cat is held by Merlin from Torquay, UK. Merlin's purr registered at 67.8 decibels, equivalent to the noise level of a vacuum cleaner.

When it comes to transport, the fastest lawnmower, crafted by Honda, can reach speeds of up to 150.99 mph. Built for sheer speed rather than yard maintenance, this lawnmower combines engineering prowess with the joy of pushing mundane objects to their limits. Perhaps even stranger, the record for the smallest roadworthy car is held by Austin Coulson's diminutive automotive creation, measuring less than 26 inches high, 25 inches wide, and just over 4 feet long, complete with all the necessary components to legally drive on public roads.

Human achievements in physical endurance present astonishing feats. Dean Karnazes, an ultramarathon runner, completed 50 marathons in 50 states in 50 consecutive days. Karnazes also ran 350 miles without sleep in 2005, showcasing not just physical endurance but extreme mental fortitude.

In the gastronomical arena, the largest pumpkin pie ever made weighed a staggering 3,699 pounds. Created by New Bremen Giant Pumpkin Growers, this dessert required 440 sheets of dough, 1,212 pounds of pumpkin, 2,796 eggs, and 109 gallons of evaporated milk to produce. Speaking of size, the largest cheeseburger, weighing 2,014 pounds, was crafted by the Black Bear Casino Resort in Carlton, Minnesota. This culinary behemoth included a 60-pound bun, a 40-pound slice of cheese, and a 50-pound serving of lettuce.

The category of human memory has its own prodigious records. Dominic O'Brien, an eight-time World Memory Champion, set a record by memorizing the order of 54 shuffled decks of playing cards after only a single viewing. This level of cognitive ability showcases the profound potential of human memory, often unattainable without extensive training and natural aptitude. Similarly, feats of mental calculation astound and defy the seemingly rigid limits of arithmetic. Shakuntala Devi, known as the "Human Computer," was capable of multiplying two 13-digit numbers in 28 seconds, a record-setting performance in its time.

Human creativity intersects with endurance in the domain of marathon music performances. The current record for the longest continuous piano concert is held by Romuald Koperski, who played for 103 hours straight. This musical marathon, besides showcasing incredible stamina, also highlights the mental and physical demands of sustained artistic performance.

Even within the realm of record-breaking, the motivations vary widely. For some, it is the pursuit of a challenge, for others a desire for recognition, and yet others might find it a way to promote a cause or bring attention to an issue. Bound by no single theme, world records find unity in the universal human urge to stretch the conceivable limits, often blending the incredible with the seemingly absurd.

31: THE PSYCHOLOGY BEHIND SUPERSTITIONS

Superstitions permeate cultures worldwide, finding expression in various forms like knocking on wood, avoiding black cats, or refraining from walking under ladders. While often dismissed as irrational, superstitions offer a glimpse into the complexities of human cognition and societal norms. Their origins can be traced back to a blend of historical, psychological, and social factors, providing both comfort and a perceived sense of control over uncertain circumstances.

Historically, superstitions often emerged in times of peril or uncertainty. Ancient civilizations, grappling with the unpredictability of life, turned to rituals and omens to provide meaning and a semblance of control. For instance, the Romans believed that the state of birds' entrails post-sacrifice could foretell the future. Such practices were not just beliefs but intertwined deeply with their cultural and spiritual lives, reflecting humanity's perpetual quest for understanding the unknown.

At a psychological level, superstitions serve as coping mechanisms in the face of uncertainty. The human brain seeks patterns and causal relationships, a tendency known as patternicity. When outcomes are unpredictable, superstitions offer a cognitive shortcut, providing a false but comforting sense of control. Behavioral psychologists describe this through the concept of "illusory correlation," where individuals link unrelated events based on their need for coherence. For example, a gambler might wear a "lucky" hat, believing it influences their odds, despite the absence of a real connection.

Superstitions also stem from the human desire for control and predictability. Cognitive dissonance theory explains how individuals reconcile contradictory beliefs and behaviors to maintain psychological consistency. Superstitious rituals become ingrained habits, reinforcing the illusion of control. This is evident in sports, where athletes engage in elaborate pre-game rituals, firmly believing they enhance performance, reducing anxiety, and bolstering confidence.

Socially, superstitions function as cultural artifacts, transmitting values and norms across generations. They often surface in shared folklore, forming a part of collective identity.

In Japan, for instance, the number four is avoided due to its phonetic similarity to the word for death. This manifests in everyday practices, such as hospitals forgoing a fourth floor. Such beliefs are woven into the fabric of cultural identity, often without questioning their origins.

Additionally, superstitions play a role in social bonding and conformity. Emile Durkheim, a founding figure in sociology, argued that shared beliefs and rituals strengthen social cohesion. Superstitions, therefore, serve as common ground, fostering a sense of belonging. Engaging in collective superstitious practices, like throwing salt over the shoulder, reinforces group identity and solidifies communal bonds.

Moreover, the persistence of superstitions in modern society can be linked to cognitive biases, particularly the availability heuristic. This bias leads individuals to overestimate the likelihood of events based on their immediate recall. If someone experiences an unusual event after breaking a mirror, they are more likely to remember and attribute it to the superstition, reinforcing the belief.

Superstitions often find fertile ground in contexts characterized by high stakes and low control. The realms of sports, gambling, and even financial markets provide fertile ground for their proliferation. Traders may rely on lucky charms during volatile market conditions, reflecting a broader human tendency to seek solace in rituals when navigating unpredictable environments.

In summary, superstitions intertwine history, psychology, and social dynamics. Far from mere irrational quirks, they offer insights into human cognition, strategies for coping with uncertainty, and mechanisms for social cohesion. While their veracity remains scientifically unsubstantiated, their enduring presence underscores fundamental aspects of the human experience.

32: THE MYSTERY OF NON-NEWTONIAN FLUIDS

In the world of fluids, Newtonian behavior, where the rate of deformation is linearly proportional to the applied stress, is a standard. Water, air, and glycerin all follow Newton's laws, complying obediently with their linear relationship between shear stress and rate of shear strain. However, in the shadow of these predictable substances exists a captivating anomaly: non-Newtonian fluids.

Non-Newtonian fluids deviate from the Newtonian norm, displaying properties and behaviors that are counterintuitive and often bizarre. These substances can act as both liquids and solids depending on the force applied to them. Their viscosity is not constant; it changes under stress. Cornstarch mixed with water, often called "Oobleck," is a quintessential example. When stirred slowly, it flows like a conventional liquid. Yet a sharp impact transforms it into a solid-like state, allowing one to walk across its surface without sinking.

The peculiarities of non-Newtonian fluids can be categorized into several types based on their distinct responses to shear stress. Shear-thickening fluids, such as the aforementioned Oobleck, increase in viscosity with the rate of shear strain. Conversely, shear-thinning fluids, like ketchup or blood, decrease in viscosity under stress, flowing more easily when agitated. This characteristic ensures that ketchup, once shaken from the bottle, pours smoothly over fries, or that blood flows readily through veins when pumped by the heart.

Thixotropic fluids add another layer of complexity. These materials, such as paint or certain clays, become less viscous over time when subjected to shear and gradually return to a more viscous state once the stress is removed. Think of paint that flows smoothly under the brush but thickens again once the strokes cease to settle into place. Rheopectic fluids are the polar opposite, gaining viscosity over time under constant shear stress, though they are far less common in everyday life.

The molecular structure or particulates dispersed within non-Newtonian fluids bestows these unusual properties. For Oobleck, cornstarch granules suspended in water interact in such a way that rapid movement forces them into close contact, creating a temporary solid network. Shear-thinning fluids rely on elongated or asymmetrical molecules, which align and streamline under stress, reducing resistance and allowing easier flow.

These unique behaviors have practical implications and applications. In the culinary world, chefs exploit shear-thinning properties to create smooth sauces and desserts. The cosmetics industry employs thixotropic gels and pastes that maintain stability in containers but spread easily when applied to skin. In biomedical engineering, non-Newtonian fluids contribute to the design of synthetic blood and adaptable prosthetic devices.

Moreover, the realm of non-Newtonian fluids extends into advanced protective gear and materials sciences. Shear-thickening fluids are integral to modern body armor, where the material remains flexible during normal movements but hardens upon impact, providing critical protection. Such technologies are instrumental for first responders and military personnel, combining comfort and defense in their wearables.

Studying non-Newtonian fluids has broader implications for understanding natural phenomena and industrial processes. The flow of magma beneath Earth's crust, the behavior of biological tissues, and the dynamics of drilling fluids in the oil industry all involve non-Newtonian behavior. This underscores the importance of non-Newtonian fluid mechanics beyond academic curiosity or laboratory experiments.

Exploring the intricacies of non-Newtonian fluids unlocks a deeper appreciation of the complexities inherent within the fluid dynamics domain, illustrating that even the most mundane substances can harbor extraordinary secrets waiting to be discovered.

33: THE HISTORICAL IMPACT OF SALT

Salt, a substance so ubiquitous today that it is present on every household kitchen table, once held a status of immense importance throughout human history. Its rarity and preservation qualities made it a highly coveted commodity, shaping economies, wars, and civilizations.

In ancient China, as early as 6000 BCE, salt harvesting from saline springs began to emerge, marking one of humanity's earliest efforts at extracting this mineral. The "salt routes" became expansive networks of trade, establishing early economic systems. It was during the Han Dynasty that government monopolies on salt transformed its trade into a significant source of state revenue, reinforcing the central power's hold on its territories.

The Egyptian civilization utilized salt not just for culinary purposes but as a critical element in the mummification process. Natron, a naturally occurring blend that included sodium carbonate and sodium bicarbonate, played a vital role in preserving the dead. The procurement and management of this resource spurred trade relations and technological developments.

In the Roman Empire, the economic and strategic importance of salt was fully realized. The word "salary" itself is derived from "salarium," a portion of payment given to Roman soldiers to buy salt. The Via Salaria, or the Salt Road, represents how integral salt was to maintaining Roman legions and, by extension, the stability and expansion of the empire.

Medieval Europe saw salt as a linchpin in the development of cities and powers. The Salt Statutes of Lübeck codified legal provisions for salt distribution in Hanseatic League towns. Salt tax, known as "gabelle" in France, was notoriously heavy and eventually contributed to the financial strain leading up to the French Revolution. The town of Salzburg, which translates to Salt Fortress, owes its name and prosperity to salt mining.

In Africa, salt's significance was evident in regions like the Sahara, where trade caravans transporting salt traversed treacherous desert routes. The exchange of gold and salt in West African empires like Mali underscored the mineral's trading power, with salt being as valuable, if not more so, than gold itself.

The Indian subcontinent provides another fascinating chapter in salt history. The British imposition of the salt tax and their control over its production exemplified colonial exploitation. Mahatma Gandhi's Salt March in 1930 highlighted the oppressive nature of British rule and became a pivotal moment in India's fight for independence, symbolizing civil disobedience and self-reliance.

Beyond its historical and economic impact, salt has played a considerable role in culinary traditions and cultural rituals. In pre-modern Japan, salt was used in Shinto purification rites and in sumo wrestling, where it was sprinkled to purify the ring. In Korea, kimchi fermentation relies heavily on salt, demonstrating the intersection of culinary innovation and salt usage.

Industrial progress also turned to salt, with its applications extending into manufacturing and chemistry. The development of the salt-chloralkali process enabled the mass production of chlorine and sodium hydroxide, chemicals crucial for modern industries ranging from paper production to pharmaceuticals.

Explorers and newcomers to various terrains discovered that salt could be a matter of survival. Salt's ability to preserve food became indispensable during long voyages and in areas devoid of other preservation methods. Ships stocked with salt fish, salt pork, and even hardtack covered in salt ensured that crews could sustain themselves over extended periods at sea, preventing malnutrition and scurvy.

Even in religious texts, salt holds metaphorical meanings. In the Bible, references to the "salt of the earth" imply worth and preservation, entwining the mineral's material value with spiritual symbolism. In similar vein, salt is used in various ceremonial contexts across cultures, signifying purity, protection, and covenant.

To this day, salt's legacy permeates our daily lives, though often unacknowledged. A condiment now taken for granted was once a cornerstone of societal development, prompting conflicts, enabling exploration, and catalyzing revolutions. Salt's journey from an irreplaceable treasure to a common staple offers a profound lens through which to understand the progression of human civilization.

34: THE INTRICACIES OF TYPOGRAPHIC DESIGN

Typographic design is often taken for granted in our visually saturated world, yet it is a field brimming with nuance and precision. At its core, typography is the art and technique of arranging type to make written language legible, readable, and visually appealing. Each typed letter is, in essence, a small piece of art—crafted with deliberate choice in style, weight, and spacing to convey a particular aesthetic and functional purpose.

Typeface, commonly conflated with font, refers to the overall design of lettering. A typeface consists of many fonts, which are specific weights and styles. For example, Helvetica forms the typeface, while Helvetica Bold or Helvetica Italic are distinct fonts within that typeface family. This distinction remains crucial among typographers whose task is to curate harmonious relationships between letters and words.

Kerning, the adjustment of space between individual letters, can significantly influence a viewer's perception of text. Proper kerning ensures that letters sit naturally next to each other, avoiding awkward gaps or unintended connections. When executed well, it imbues a subtle sense of order and professionalism to the text, whether in print or digital media.

Leading, another key typographic term, delineates the vertical space between lines of text. Named from the bygone days of hand-setting type, when thin strips of lead were placed between lines, modern leading controls readability and can dramatically alter the visual density of a text block. A tight leading can create a sense of urgency or compactness, while loose leading imparts an airy, open feel.

Tracking, similar to kerning but applied to groups of letters, adjusts the overall space across a block of text. This uniform letter-spacing technique can change the texture and tone of text, making it visually lighter or heavier. Increased tracking can impart a sense of elegance and formality or enhance the legibility of all-caps text, which can often appear crowded without adjustment.

The choice of typeface itself can evoke historical, emotional, and practical associations. Serif fonts, with their small projecting features at the end of strokes, often suggest tradition, reliability, and formality. Classic examples include Times New Roman and Garamond. In contrast, sans-serif fonts like Arial and Helvetica, which lack these decorative strokes, convey modernity and simplicity.

Hand-drawn or script typefaces, resembling cursive handwriting, offer a personal, intimate feel. Their fluid, organic shapes can imbue a design with warmth and elegance. Yet, they are generally reserved for headlines or decorative use, as extended text in script can be difficult to read.

Beyond aesthetic considerations, the functional aspect of typography plays a critical role in accessibility and user experience. Legibility under varied viewing conditions—whether on small mobile screens, billboards, or in dim lighting—is paramount. Typeface designers painstakingly craft each character to ensure clarity at different sizes and resolutions.

Typography's history is rich with cultural shifts and technological advancements. The invention of movable type by Johannes Gutenberg in the 15th century revolutionized print, enabling mass communication and democratizing access to information. Subsequent centuries saw the rise of myriad typographic styles, each reflective of its era's social and technological context. The Industrial Revolution, for example, precipitated bold, eye-catching typefaces to cater to advertising's growing demand.

In the digital age, typography continues to evolve. Variable fonts, an emerging technology, allow designers to adjust a typeface's weight, width, and other attributes dynamically, paving the way for adaptable and responsive typography across diverse media.

Despite the omnipresence of text in our lives, the intricacies of typographic design remain a largely unseen art form. Its subtleties influence not just how we read, but how we perceive and engage with the world around us. In every billboard, book, and web page, typography quietly shapes our visual landscape, balancing art and science to enhance the written word's clarity and impact.

35: THE INTRIGUING WORLD OF SYNESTHESIA

Synesthesia is a neurological phenomenon where stimulation of one sensory pathway leads to involuntary experiences in another sensory pathway. Considered a blending of the senses, synesthetes might perceive letters as inherently colored or hear sounds that invoke vivid tastes. This extraordinary sensory cross-wiring can transform mundane experiences into multisensory adventures.

Grapheme-color synesthesia is one of the most common forms, where individuals see specific letters or numbers in certain colors. For example, the letter "A" might always appear as red, while "B" might look blue. This association remains consistent over time, showing a stability that differentiates it from simple mnemonic aids. Lexical-gustatory synesthesia, though rarer, causes individuals to taste specific flavors when they hear particular words. A synesthete with this type might find that the name "Jane" tastes like lemon.

The neurological underpinnings of synesthesia are not fully understood, but many researchers believe it results from increased communication between adjacent sensory areas in the brain. Functional MRI (fMRI) studies have shown that when synesthetes perceive stimuli triggering their synesthesia, areas of the brain corresponding to both the triggering and the associated sensation become activated. This cross-activation theory suggests that the phenomenon might stem from a unique pattern of neural connections established during development.

Remarkably, synesthesia might actually enhance cognitive abilities in specific domains. Many synesthetes report that their cross-sensory experiences aid memory and creativity. The vivid sensory associations can make it easier to recall names, dates, or numbers. Some research even suggests that synesthetes have enhanced perceptual discrimination abilities, as the consistent sensory associations can act as an additional layer of information processing.

Historical records indicate that synesthesia is not a modern discovery. Notable individuals, including composer Franz Liszt and physicist Richard Feynman, purportedly experienced synesthetic perceptions. Liszt, for instance, would instruct his orchestra to play a section "more blue" or "deep violet." Recognition of this condition in famous creative minds hints at a potential link between synesthesia and artistic or intellectual genius.

The prevalence of synesthesia varies widely in academic estimates but generally ranges between 1 in 2,000 to 1 in 20 people. This wide disparity is partly due to varying awareness and self-reporting among those who have the condition. Synesthesia-tracking tools and rigorous diagnostic criteria continue to evolve, allowing researchers to better understand its distribution and characteristics within the general population.

Interestingly, synesthesia often runs in families, suggesting a genetic component. Genetics studies have identified several candidate genes that might contribute to the condition. Although no single "synesthesia gene" has been discovered, the heritable nature implies a complex genetic architecture. This discovery hints at broader questions about the genetic bases of perception and cognitive diversity.

Cultural and individual variability adds another layer of intrigue. Specific synesthetic associations can be influenced by personal experiences and cultural context. One synesthete's "C" might be turquoise, while another's might be chartreuse. Additionally, the condition appears to arise more frequently in individuals who exhibit heightened levels of sensory processing sensitivity, confirming that variation in perceptual experiences extends across a spectrum.

While synesthesia is generally benign, some individuals might find it overwhelming, especially when the sensory inputs are strong or frequent. For most, however, it enriches life in unexpected ways, adding a layer of sensory embellishment to everyday activities. The phenomenon also invites broader contemplation about the nature of human perception, the boundaries of sensory experience, and the neurological diversity that characterizes cognitive functioning.

Research continues to unveil the mechanisms and implications of this fascinating condition, expanding our understanding of how the brain constructs and interprets reality.

36: THE SCIENCE OF MEMORY

Memory, often perceived as a simple act of recalling past experiences, is a complex and multifaceted mental function. It entails a series of processes by which information is encoded, stored, and retrieved, forming the backbone of our cognitive capabilities. Encoded information passes through multiple stages, specifically sensory memory, short-term memory, and long-term memory.

Sensory memory is the initial, extremely brief capture of sensory information from our environment. This type of memory is subdivided into iconic memory for visual information and echoic memory for auditory information. These fleeting impressions typically last for a fraction of a second to a few seconds, providing a buffer that allows the brain to process and interpret sensory data.

Short-term memory, often referred to as working memory, holds information for a short period—typically around 20 to 30 seconds. This stage of memory is crucial for performing everyday tasks, such as remembering a phone number long enough to dial it. Working memory has a limited capacity, often cited as being able to hold about seven items at once, a concept known as Miller's Law. Rehearsal techniques, such as chunking, can enhance the retention of information in this stage.

Long-term memory is where information is stored more permanently, ranging from periods of several hours to a lifetime. This type of memory is categorized into explicit (or declarative) memory and implicit (or non-declarative) memory. Explicit memory involves the conscious recall of information, which is further divided into episodic memory (specific events and experiences) and semantic memory (general knowledge and facts). Implicit memory, on the other hand, involves unconscious memory skills and conditioned responses.

The encoding of information into long-term memory is a dynamic and selective process. It often depends on the depth of processing, which refers to the level of engagement and attention devoted to the information being learned. Deep processing, involving semantic and meaningful analysis, typically results in stronger memory traces compared to shallow processing, which involves mere surface-level analysis.

The hippocampus, a structure located within the brain's medial temporal lobe, plays a pivotal role in the formation and organization of new memories. It acts as a sort of memory indexer, sending information to various parts of the brain for storage and retrieval when necessary. Damage to the hippocampus can result in severe impairments, such as anterograde amnesia, where an individual is unable to form new memories.

The consolidation of memories, a process that transforms transient short-term memories into stable long-term ones, involves the interplay of synaptic and systemic mechanisms. Synaptic consolidation occurs within the first few hours after learning, as synaptic connections between neurons are strengthened. Systemic consolidation can take days, months, or even years, as memories are gradually transferred from the hippocampus to more distributed networks in the cortex.

Retrieval, the process of accessing stored information, can be influenced by various factors, including the context in which the information was encoded and the retrieval cues present at the time of recall. The encoding specificity principle suggests that memories are more easily recalled when the context at retrieval closely matches the context at encoding. Similarly, state-dependent memory indicates that information learned in a specific physiological or emotional state is more easily retrieved when one is in that same state.

However, memory is not infallible. Factors such as decay, interference, and retrieval failures can lead to forgetting. Decay theory posits that memory traces weaken over time, while interference theory suggests that other information can disrupt the recall of specific memories. Retroactive interference occurs when new information hinders the recall of older information, whereas proactive interference involves older memories interfering with the encoding of new information.

Distortions and false memories further complicate the accuracy of our recollections. Memories are reconstructive in nature and can be influenced by suggestive questioning, misinformation, and the integration of imaginative elements. The misinformation effect, for instance, demonstrates how exposure to incorrect information can alter an individual's memory of an event.

The study of memory extends into numerous fields, including psychology, neuroscience, and cognitive science, each contributing to a deeper understanding of how memories are formed, stored, and retrieved. From the molecular mechanisms that facilitate synaptic changes to the psychological principles guiding mnemonic strategies, the science of memory continues to be a rich and evolving area of research.

37: THE MYSTIQUE OF TIME CAPSULES

The concept of a time capsule encapsulates humanity's desire to communicate with the future. These treasures of the past are containers filled with artifacts, messages, and memorabilia intended for discovery by future generations. Time capsules can be as modest as a small personal box buried in a backyard or as grand as projects undertaken by entire communities, organizations, and even governments.

The cornerstone ceremony for a time capsule typically includes a public gathering, where individuals contribute items deemed representative of the era. These items range from everyday objects like newspapers, photographs, and coins to more personalized memorabilia such as letters and artworks. The selection process is weighted with the responsibility of capturing the essence of a specific time period, acting as a historical snapshot for those who will eventually unearth it.

The International Time Capsule Society, established in 1990, is dedicated to the study and documentation of time capsules worldwide. According to their records, thousands of time capsules are buried globally, yet many are forgotten over time. Often, these capsules are discovered accidentally during construction activities or excavation projects, revealing their contents decades or even centuries later.

The Crypt of Civilization, located at Oglethorpe University in Georgia, USA, is one of the most ambitious time capsules to date. Sealed in 1940, it is intended to be opened in the year 8113. The crypt contains microfilm, artifacts, and documentation that convey the cultural, scientific, and social milieu of the early 20th century. Items range from everyday tools to technical gadgets and literary works, aiming to provide a comprehensive representation of contemporary life.

In contrast, the Westinghouse Time Capsules, created for the 1939 and 1964 New York World Fairs, focus on technological progress and cultural milestones. These capsules, scheduled for retrieval in the year 6939, house items such as a slide rule, a newsreel of the World Fair, and a package of Camel cigarettes. These selections offer a glimpse into mid-20th century Americana, emphasizing the era's technological optimism.

The KEO satellite project, an international endeavor, aims to encapsulate messages from humanity. Scheduled for launch by 2022, it will orbit the Earth for 50,000 years before returning. Individuals worldwide can contribute messages that encompass personal reflections, hopes, and experiences. The KEO project exemplifies the universal nature of the time capsule concept, transcending geographical and cultural boundaries.

Time capsules serve not only as historical archives but also provoke philosophical reflections. They challenge us to think about how future generations will perceive our era and how our actions and artifacts will be interpreted. They compel us to consider the evolution of technology, culture, and society over spans of time far exceeding human lifetimes.

School groups frequently participate in time capsule projects, providing students with a unique educational experience. The process fosters a sense of continuity, linking the students' present experience with the future. It encourages them to reflect on what items truly represent their current lives and contemplate how drastically the world might change by the time the capsule is reopened.

In 2014, a time capsule buried by Paul Revere and Samuel Adams in 1795 was unearthed in Boston. The capsule contained newspapers, coins, and a silver plaque, offering a tangible connection to America's early history. Such discoveries provide historians with invaluable primary sources, offering unique insights into the period's cultural and political climate.

However, the preservation of time capsules poses significant challenges. Potential hazards include environmental deterioration, contamination, and human forgetfulness. Effective time capsules require careful planning, including selecting resilient materials, choosing burial sites with minimal risk of disturbance, and documenting precise locations to ensure future retrieval.

In contemporary culture, digital time capsules have emerged, leveraging technology to capture and store data for future access. These digital repositories include video recordings, digital photographs, and even social media posts, preserved in formats intended to withstand the rapid evolution of technology. These virtual capsules underscore the changing nature of how we document and preserve human experience in the digital age.

Time capsules epitomize the intersection of history, culture, and human aspiration. They act as bridges between eras, offering a preserved glimpse into the occasions and emotions that characterized past generations. As relics designed with the intent of future discovery, they continuously ignite curiosity and provide a profound sense of connection through time.

38: BIZARRE FORMS OF PRECIPITATION

Precipitation, in general, is commonly understood as rain or snow, but the atmospheric conditions on Earth can produce far more unusual and varied forms. One of the rarest and arguably most dramatic occurrences is the phenomenon of raining frogs or fish. Documented instances throughout history reveal that during powerful storms, small aquatic animals can be swept into waterspouts or tornadoes, transported over land, and then fall back to the ground, creating bizarre showers that surprise and perplex witnesses.

Hailstorms can also present extraordinary characteristics. Although typically composed of spherical ice pellets, hailstones can vary significantly in size and shape. It's not uncommon for hailstones to amalgamate into jagged, irregular shapes through repeated cycles of updrafts and downdrafts within a thunderstorm. These unusually shaped hailstones can cause significant agricultural damage and pose dangers to both animals and humans.

Another fascinating type of precipitation is blood rain, which has piqued curiosity and fear across various cultures. Contemporary scientific understanding attributes this phenomenon to the presence of red-colored dust or microorganisms, such as microalgae, suspended in raindrops. These particles can derive from distinct geographical sources, like dust storms in the Sahara Desert, which then get transported across vast distances by atmospheric currents, eventually mixing with rain clouds and coloring the precipitation red.

In colder climates, diamond dust represents one of the most enchanting types of precipitation. This meteorological event occurs under clear-sky conditions, typically at temperatures below -30°C (-22°F), and consists of tiny ice crystals that sparkle in the sunlight. Diamond dust is especially prevalent in polar regions and high-altitude areas and can contribute to rare optical phenomena like halos and light pillars.

Sleet and freezing rain, while more common, manifest unique physical transitions between rain and snow. Sleet occurs when raindrops freeze into ice pellets before reaching the ground, while freezing rain results when supercooled raindrops make contact with surfaces, instantly forming a glaze of ice. Both sleet and freezing rain can lead to hazardous travel conditions and significant structural damages.

Snow itself can manifest in unusual forms, with thundersnow being one prominent example. Thundersnow is a rare weather event where thunderstorms produce snow instead of rain. The combination of lightning, thunder, and heavy snowfall creates a dramatic and uncommon spectacle, often accompanied by severe winter conditions.

Color and texture variations in snow can also occur. In polar and high-altitude environments, snow can be tinted by naturally occurring algae, resulting in phenomena such as watermelon snow, which appears pink and has a faint scent resembling watermelon. Furthermore, snow rollers are naturally occurring cylindrical snow formations shaped by wind and gravity. These rare structures are formed when the right combination of moisture and wind conditions causes snow to gather and roll into cylindrical shapes.

The diversity of precipitation types continues with volcanic ash or tephra fallout during volcanic eruptions. When a volcano erupts, the explosive discharge of ash, pumice, and other volcanic materials can be carried by wind currents over considerable distances, eventually falling back to the ground as ash rain. This type of precipitation, while visually striking, is a significant hazard, capable of disrupting agriculture, causing respiratory issues, and damaging machinery and infrastructure.

Lastly, manna or mysterious substances falling from the sky have been subjects of historical and contemporary intrigue. Historically, accounts describe manna as a divine substance provided as food, often associated with biblical narratives. In modern times, such mysterious falls are frequently attributed to natural phenomena like lichen combined with environmental factors, offering plausible explanations for what ancient civilizations may have perceived as miraculous.

39: THE MECHANICS OF CAT PURRING

Cats have been companions to humans for thousands of years, yet certain aspects of their physiology remain shrouded in mystery. One such enigma is the purring mechanism. The purr, a sound both soothing and intriguing, has led to numerous studies and theories, none of which have definitively explained the entire phenomenon.

To comprehend the mechanics of cat purring, one must first understand the anatomical structures involved. Cats produce the sound of a purr due to the rapid, rhythmic contractions of the laryngeal muscles located in their voice boxes, or larynges. These muscles oscillate both during inhalation and exhalation, resulting in a continuous sound. Unlike other cat vocalizations, which occur only during exhalation, the purr happens during both phases of breathing.

The primary muscles involved, particularly the thyroarytenoid muscles, work in conjunction with a neural oscillator in the cat's brain. This oscillator sends periodic neural signals to the laryngeal muscles, instructing them to contract at a rate that typically ranges from 25 to 150 vibrations per second, or Hertz. This frequency varies slightly among different cat species and individual cats. The vibrations cause a sudden, intermittent separation of the vocal cords, producing a series of short bursts of sound. These bursts are what we recognize as a purr.

Purring can begin as early as when kittens are just a few days old, which raises the question of its purpose and evolution. Initially, it may serve a practical role: fostering a bond between the mother cat and her offspring. The nearly continuous purring of kittens, even as they nurse, may reassure the mother of their wellbeing. This vocalization's low volume and constant nature make it ideal for such close-quarter communication.

Adult cat purring, however, serves broader purposes. Commonly associated with contentment, cats purr when they are relaxed and comfortable, often in their owner's lap or in a sunbeam. Yet cats also purr under circumstances that do not immediately suggest happiness, such as when they are in pain, frightened, or even during labor. This duality hints at a more complex set of functions behind the purr. One prevailing theory suggests that purring may have a self-soothing or analgesic effect, helping cats to calm themselves in stressful or painful situations.

Further research has proposed that purring frequencies might also play a role in healing. Some studies suggest that the vibrations produced at specific Hertz ranges might promote tissue regeneration and bone healing. These findings have spurred curiosity about the purr's potential therapeutic applications, not just for cats but also for other animals and even humans.

Another utilitarian application of the purr is its role in communication. Cats often purr to capture human attention or solicit food and affection. This aspect of purring illustrates the intricate social dynamics between domesticated cats and their human companions. The specific frequency and amplitude of a purr can vary depending on what the cat seeks to communicate, and keen observers can often distinguish between a purr for contentment and one soliciting interaction.

Despite the multitude of studies on the topic, the definitive biological and evolutionary purposes of purring remain elusive. The complexity embedded in this seemingly simple sound serves as a reminder of the broader mysteries within the animal kingdom and our understanding of interspecies communication. Though we may not yet fully grasp the mechanics or full range of functions behind the purr, it remains one of the endearing—and enigmatic—traits of our feline companions.

40: THE PHYSICS OF SOAP BUBBLES

Soap bubbles, with their dazzling iridescence and delicate fragility, are deceptively simple. The creation of a soap bubble starts with a thin layer of soapy water sandwiching a layer of air. This structure, known as a soap film, exhibits remarkable properties due to surface tension—a force resulting from the cohesive nature of water molecules. When air is blown into this film, it expands to minimize its surface area, forming a spherical shape.

The colors of soap bubbles are a result of light interference. When light hits a soap bubble, some of it reflects off the outer surface while another part enters the film, reflecting off the inner surface. The two sets of reflected light waves interfere with each other. Depending on the thickness of the film and the wavelength of the light, this can enhance or cancel out certain colors, resulting in the shifting, rainbow-like hues seen on bubbles.

Gravity affects soap bubbles by causing the liquid film to drain downward, making the top thinner than the bottom. As the film thins, it becomes more prone to rupture. The smallest disturbance—whether from a dust particle or the evaporation of water—can cause the bubble to burst. Evaporation also plays a crucial role in the lifetime of a bubble, as the water in the film makes it evaporates continually until the film is too thin to hold the bubble's shape.

The science behind the soap bubble extends further into the study of minimal surfaces—a concept in mathematics describing surfaces that minimize their area given certain constraints. Soap films are natural examples of minimal surfaces because they adjust themselves to the least possible area for a given volume of air inside. This principle is applied in various fields like architecture and material science to design efficient structures and materials.

The interactions between soap molecules and water molecules explain much of the bubble's physics. Soap molecules are amphiphilic, meaning they have a hydrophilic (water-attracting) head and a hydrophobic (water-repelling) tail. When soap is mixed with water, these molecules arrange themselves into a bilayer. This formation decreases the surface tension of water, allowing the creation of flexible, stable films that can stretch into bubbles.

Despite their simplicity, soap bubbles can serve as models for more complex scientific phenomena. For example, the study of soap films has provided insights into fluid dynamics, hydrodynamics, and even topology. Bubbles have practical applications in technology and industry, such as in the development of lightweight, strong materials or in processes like froth flotation for mineral extraction.

Soap bubbles' fleeting existence makes them a subject of fascination not only for children but also for scientists. Their formation, vibrant colors, and eventual burst are governed by fundamental principles of physics and chemistry that illustrate the intricate balance of forces at play in nature.

41: THE SECRET LIFE OF WORDS

Languages are living organisms, evolving and adapting over time. The journey a word takes can be unexpected, shifting in meaning, crossing cultural boundaries, and acquiring new nuances. Take the word "silly," for example. In its Old English roots, it was "seely," meaning happy or fortunate. Over the centuries, through a complex interplay of usage and context, it transformed into a term for something trivial or foolish. Such shifts are neither linear nor always logical; they mirror the dynamic and ever-changing nature of human societies.

The blending of cultures often results in delightful linguistic mutations. Consider "algebra," a field of mathematics. The term derives from the Arabic word "al-jabr," meaning the reunion of broken parts, a nod to its origins in the works of Persian mathematicians. Likewise, the intricate patterns of Romanesque architecture gave name to "rococo," derived from "rocaille," the French word for shell-covered rockwork, an emblem of the often convoluted journey of terms across time and geography.

A fascinating example of linguistic evolution can be found in the word "quirky." Its etymological path winds back to the Middle English "querken," meaning to turn or twist. Over time, it was adapted to describe something peculiar or eccentric. How did this transformation occur? One can speculate, but its path is as unpredictable as the very concept it now signifies.

Words also carry with them stories of cultural exchange. "Ketchup," now an almost universal condiment, finds its origin in the Hokkien Chinese word "kê-tsiap," a type of fermented fish sauce. This term traveled through Malay and English trading routes before landing on Western tables, where it transformed into the tomato-based sauce we recognize today. The cross-pollination of languages through travel, trade, and conquest leaves its mark indelibly on the words we use.

A particularly illustrative case is the term "nightmare." In Old English, a "mare" was an evil spirit believed to sit on people's chests while they slept, causing bad dreams. This belief was so prevalent that the term persisted into modern times, even as its ethereal association faded. The melding of myth and language anchors parts of our lexicon in the distant superstitions of our ancestors.

Shakespeare, often hailed as one of the greatest influencers of the English language, coined or popularized an estimated 1,700 words, many of which remain in use. Phrases like "break the ice," "heart of gold," and "wild-goose chase" first appeared in his works, showcasing the creative potential of language manipulation. Each phrase carries with it the bard's unique emotional and narrative contexts, revealing how literature can shape and morph the vernacular.

The term "berserk" traces back to the Old Norse "berserkr," describing Norse warriors who fought with wild, animalistic fury, perhaps under the influence of intoxicants or bound by ritualistic fervor. Over centuries, as tales of Viking valor and terror filtered into broader European consciousness, "berserk" found its way into English, encapsulating a sense of uncontrolled rage. The transformation carries echoes of ancient battles, fusing them with contemporary understanding.

Sometimes, words journey through language with subtle yet profound cultural shifts. "Robot," coined by Czech writer Karel Čapek in his 1920 play "R.U.R." (Rossum's Universal Robots), springs from "robota," the Czech word for forced labor. This term encapsulated early 20th-century anxieties about industrialization and automation, encapsulating fears that remain potent in modern times. Its etymological path underscores how new concepts in technology necessitate new linguistic expressions.

Another striking example is "sarcasm," whose etymology traverses the Greek word "sarkazein," meaning to tear flesh like dogs. This imagery vividly conveys the cutting, sometimes vicious nature of sarcastic remarks, pointing to the power of words to wound emotionally as well as inform. The term's evolution from a visceral act to a verbal one highlights the metaphorical leaps language can make.

Exploring the lineage of words reveals the rich tapestry of human interaction, blending mythology, reality, emotion, and intellect. Each word is a thread in a vast, intricate web of communication, echoing the myriad ways humans perceive and understand their world. Through understanding the secret life of words, one gains not only insights into language but also a deeper appreciation for the diverse and complex history it encompasses. The pathways words travel illuminate the shadowy corridors of human thought, culture, and history, adding layers of meaning and connection to even the most mundane conversations.

42: THE PECULIARITIES OF ANIMAL BEHAVIOR

On the dark, murky floor of the ocean, a small cuttlefish prepares for what could be the most crucial performance of its life. With a flicker of bioluminescence, it begins to weave an intricate light show, morphing its skin into a display of colors and patterns that are both mesmerizing and baffling. The object of its attention, a nearby cuttlefish of the opposite sex, is either suitably impressed or completely unfazed—it is often difficult to gauge. This curious display is but one example in the vast, intricate tapestry of peculiar animal behaviors observed in the natural world.

In the dry, desolate stretches of the Namib Desert, the fog-basking beetle exhibits a bizarre yet effective survival strategy. Relying on the scant moisture provided by the morning fog, the beetle assumes a posture with its rear end angled upward. Tiny droplets of water condense on its back, rolling down toward its mouth, ensuring hydration in an environment where water is a precious commodity. This behavior, seemingly simple, underscores a profound adaptation to a hostile climate.

Switching to the snow-laden environs of the Arctic, the dishonest practices of the Arctic fox reveal another layer of animal cunning. These opportunistic predators have been known to follow polar bears, lying in wait as the larger bruin makes a kill. Recognizing the bear's formidable prowess, the fox seizes the opportunity to scavenge leftovers, a resourceful survival strategy that requires minimal effort and risk. In this harsh, frigid world, survival often demands resourcefulness over brute strength.

In the winding rivers of the Amazon Basin, the electric eel flaunts its ability to generate electrical discharges. With organs evolved specifically for this purpose, the eel can deliver shocks up to 600 volts—enough to stun prey or deter predators. This electrogenic capability illustrates an extraordinary evolutionary path in which electric fields conquer a watery domain more effectively than tooth and claw.

Shift focus to the palaces of peafowl and their elaborate courtship displays. Male peafowls, or peacocks, spread their iridescent tail feathers in a fan-like array that shimmers with an array of vibrant colors. This extravagant display is not merely for show; it plays a crucial role in sexual selection. Females, or peahens, scrutinize these peacock plumes, engaging in a form of vetting that is both visual and instinctual. The more impressive the display, the higher the likelihood of mating success, a testament to the intricate dance of natural selection.

Meanwhile, across the globe, the bowerbird constructs architectural marvels to attract a mate. Unlike the utilitarian nests of most birds, the bowerbird's creation is a bona fide work of art. Using twigs, leaves, and an assortment of colorful objects—everything from berries to pieces of plastic—the male bowerbird creates a structure designed to captivate the female's attention. It's a painstaking process, mirroring human architectural endeavors, albeit on a miniature scale.

In the dense jungles of Papua New Guinea, the Vogelkop gardener bowerbird takes it even further. Not satisfied with mere structure, this bird meticulously arranges a garden around its bower, collecting flowers, fruits, and even fungus to create an aesthetically pleasing array that entices a potential mate. The dedication to this complex and visually appealing construction digresses significantly from the more direct approaches seen in the animal kingdom, showing a nuanced form of attraction and competition.

In the chilly waters surrounding Antarctica, emperor penguins engage in an arduous and communal reproductive behavior. After the often treacherous trek to their breeding grounds, the female lays a single egg, which she promptly transfers to the male. The male then assumes the role of primary caregiver, balancing the egg on his feet and shielding it with a flap of skin known as a brood pouch. For months, the males huddle together to keep warm while fasting, demonstrating a communal survival strategy that underscores both sacrifice and cooperation.

Moving to the tropical canopies, one encounters the elaborate rituals of the satin bowerbird. This avian Casanova crafts meticulously decorated bowers, structures not meant for shelter but rather as a stage for showcasing collected blue items ranging from flowers to pen lids. Beyond its architectural interests, the bird engages in performance art, using dances and vocalizations to further entice mates. The extent of creativity and effort speaks volumes about the complexities of sexual selection in the wild.

Descending into the burrows of the naked mole-rat, one discovers a social organization akin to that of eusocial insects like bees and ants. These subterranean mammals live in colonies dominated by a single breeding queen and her consorts, while other members of the colony assume roles as workers or soldiers. This unusual social structure allows for remarkable cooperative behaviors, including the sharing of food and collective defense, contributing to the colony's overall survival and resilience in their challenging subterranean habitat.

Whether it is the deceptive mimicry of the cuckoo bird, which lays its eggs in the nests of unsuspecting host species, or the synchronized flashing of fireflies in a tropical swarm, the animal kingdom brims with behaviors that defy simplistic explanations. Even the enigmatic narwhal, with its elongated tusk spiraling like a unicorn's horn, invites curiosity regarding its precise function—ranging from tool use to social status signaling.

    These peculiarities illustrate an endlessly diverse spectrum of behaviors, each with its own blend of complexity, ingenuity, and sometimes sheer oddity. The more we delve into the world of animal behavior, the more it becomes apparent that these quirky strategies, whether in service of survival, reproduction, or social interaction, offer invaluable insights into the adaptive capabilities of life on Earth.

43: THE HISTORY OF ODD INVENTIONS

Human history is replete with remarkable innovation, yet some inventions stand out solely for their inexplicability. These creations, perhaps more than any mainstream technological triumph, reflect the boundless curiosity and eccentricity of the human spirit.

One such invention is the cat piano, a whimsical yet disturbing musical device that traces its origins to the 17th century. The instrument consists of a series of cats arranged with their tails aligned to a keyboard. When a key is pressed, a mechanism pulls on the corresponding tail, resulting in a diverse ensemble of meows and yowls. This curious contraption is attributed to Athanasius Kircher, a German Jesuit scholar who dabbled in various disciplines. Kircher believed in blending science and art, even if it meant resorting to peculiar methods. While there is no substantial evidence that such an instrument was ever constructed, its conception is a testament to the extremes of human inventiveness.

Not all odd inventions remained in the realm of folklore. Consider the Double Umbrella from the 19th century, designed to provide shelter for two people simultaneously. This contraption featured a wooden stick with a canopy at each end, ensuring that couples could stroll together in the rain without jostling for space under a single umbrella. Practicality aside, the double umbrella never soared in popularity, perhaps because of its unwieldy nature or the awkwardness it imposed on users negotiating their paths.

Another outlandish invention is the Portable Folding Bridge by Hormusjee Naorojee Mody in the late 1800s. Attempting to solve the logistical challenges faced by railways in India during the monsoon season, Mody conceived a collapsing bridge that could be carried by elephants. While commendable for its ingenuity, the bridge struggled with the technical limitations of its time—a lack of suitable materials and cumbersome deployment process. Although Mody received patents and admiration for his project, engineering practicalities prevented its widespread implementation.

Then there's the cigarette umbrella, patented in 1931, aimed at ensuring smokers could light and enjoy their cigarettes amidst inclement weather. Embodying both the era's fondness for smoking and a dogged determination to curb nature's interference, this device featured an umbrella attached to an extendable holder to keep cigarettes dry. Despite its functional premise, it never transcended into a common accessory. Perhaps the oddity of combining smoking paraphernalia with weather gear simply did not capture the public's imagination.

In the early 20th century, aviation pioneer Sir George Cayley designed an artificially buoyant dress meant to ensure safety in water despite its contrivance from standard fabric. Dubbed the "Aerial Lifesaver," the dress incorporated an air bladder sewn into the fabric, granting the wearer buoyancy. Brilliant and lifesaving in concept, it failed to gain traction due to the eclectic style discrepancies and the lack of marketing toward the broader public.

The 1950s saw the rise of an invention with retrofuturistic charm: the Walking Wheels by Joseph F. Beamish. The wheels, retrofitted with multiple legs, moved in a walking motion rather than a rolling one. Beamish envisioned his Walking Wheels as a revolutionary improvement in wheel technology, promising better stability and rough terrain traversal. Yet, the complexity and inefficiency of the design compared to the simplicity of traditional wheels relegated this invention to mere novelty.

Another creation of interest is the Chess-Playing Turk, an 18th-century automaton that purportedly played chess against human opponents. Invented by Wolfgang von Kempelen, the Turk was a life-sized figure dressed in Turkish robes, complete with a mechanical arm to move chess pieces. It toured Europe, defeating numerous challengers and astonishing audiences, including luminaries like Napoleon Bonaparte and Benjamin Franklin. However, the Turk's secret lay in its concealed human chess master, whose presence remained hidden behind intricate mechanisms. Though ultimately revealed as a hoax, the Turk captivated the public's fascination with automata and prefigured the complex relationships between humans and machines.

A quite different concept comes to us from Otis Tufts in the 1860s. His Steam Man was a steam-powered humanoid machine conceived to assist in heavy lifting tasks. Standing over six feet tall, this iron behemoth was reportedly capable of various feats of strength and mobility. However, the practical challenges of heat, weight, and control meant that the Steam Man remained largely an exhibition piece rather than a functional marvel of the industrial age.

In a stranger twist still, the 1980s saw the advent of the Doodleburger, an attempt at high-speed hamburger preparation through the amalgamation of mechanized assembly and culinary processes. Born amidst fast-food frenzy, the Doodleburger machine sought to substitute human cooks with a singular device capable of grilling, assembling, and wrapping hamburgers. Despite the novelty and promise of rapid food preparation, the Doodleburger encountered insurmountable issues in quality control and hygiene, terminating its potential to revolutionize the food industry.

This tapestry of odd inventions underscores humanity's relentless and sometimes whimsical quest for knowledge and improvement, even when practicality yields to imagination. Each of these inventions, though peculiar, illuminates the inventors' distinctive approaches to problem-solving, no matter how abstract or implausible those problems might appear.

44: ECCENTRIC HISTORICAL FIGURES

Throughout history, certain individuals have stood out not only for their achievements but often for their peculiar behavior and unconventional lifestyles. These figures captivate our curiosity, primarily because their eccentricities defy the norms of their respective eras. Take, for instance, Grigori Rasputin. Born a peasant in late 19th-century Russia, Rasputin rose to inexplicable influence over the Romanov family, especially Tsarina Alexandra. His purported mystical abilities and control over the hemophiliac heir, Alexei, created a mythos around him that married faith healing with dark superstition. Rasputin's murder—a convoluted affair involving poison, shooting, and drowning—only added to the aura of a man whose life seemed a constant, baffling enigma.

Then there is Joshua Norton, who declared himself Emperor Norton I of the United States in 1859. Though considered mad by many, Emperor Norton became a beloved figure in San Francisco, where he issued decrees, "proclaimed" reforms, and even "abolished" Congress. Unsurprisingly, none of his decrees ever had any legal standing, yet his eccentricity earned him a special, enduring affection from the citizens. He was granted free meals and front-row seats at events, and upon his death in 1880, some 10,000 people attended his funeral, a testament to the magnetic pull of his odd reign.

Mad King Ludwig II of Bavaria, who ruled in the mid-to-late 19th century, was equally unconventional. An introvert with a penchant for grandiose architectural projects, Ludwig neglected affairs of state to build his fairy-tale castles like Neuschwanstein, which now attract millions of visitors annually. Known for his isolation and obsession with the operas of Richard Wagner, Ludwig's actions became increasingly erratic until he was declared insane. His mysterious death in the shallow waters of Lake Starnberg added a tragic, even conspiratorial, note to his bizarre legacy, blending regal power with the escapism of personal fantasy.

Equally fascinating is the life of Nikola Tesla, a man whose scientific brilliance was matched by his idiosyncrasies. Tesla had an obsessive fear of germs and an aversion to pearls; he reportedly refused to speak to women wearing them. Known for working late into the night and indulging in powerful visualizations of his inventions, Tesla claimed to receive vivid flashes of inspiration. Despite his groundbreaking work in alternating current (AC) and wireless electricity, he ended his life penniless, feeding pigeons in New York City, illustrating the precarious balance between genius and madness.

Wilhelm Reich, another figure of great controversy and eccentricity, was a psychoanalyst who studied under Sigmund Freud but later proposed theories so outlandish they alienated him from the scientific community. Reich believed in "orgone energy," a life force he claimed could be harnessed for healing. He built "orgone accumulators" that he asserted could cure diseases and enhance vitality. Wanted by the FDA for making unfounded medical claims, Reich died in prison, but his peculiar theories continue to attract a fringe following.

Aleister Crowley, known as "the wickedest man in the world," took the realm of spiritual eccentricity to grandiose heights. An occultist, writer, and mountaineer, Crowley founded the religion of Thelema, dictating that adherents should "Do what thou wilt." His life was a maelstrom of ritual magic, drug experiments, and sexual escapades, making him a notorious figure even beyond the occult community. His presence infused the fringes of society with a strange blend of intellect and esoteric chaos.

Another outlandish figure is Queen Christina of Sweden, who abdicated her throne in 1654. A polymath, Christina invited philosophers like René Descartes to her court, cultivating an atmosphere of intellectual rigor. Her tendency to dress in men's clothing and shun marriage led to rumors and speculation, further amplified by her conversion to Catholicism and subsequent move to Rome, a drastic change from her Protestant upbringing. Her life defies the simplistic narratives often ascribed to women of her time, blending scholarly pursuits with theatrical provocations.

Lastly, Diogenes of Sinope, a philosopher of ancient Greece, embodied eccentricity through his extreme cynicism. Eschewing material comforts, Diogenes lived in a large ceramic jar and carried a lantern in daylight, claiming to be searching for an honest man. His blatant disregard for societal norms extended to all aspects of his life, including defacing currency and sabotaging public conversations. Despite—or perhaps because of—his scorn for convention, Diogenes left a lasting intellectual legacy through his teachings and extreme individualism.

45: STRANGE PHENOMENA IN NATURE

Nature, in its unbridled majesty, holds a repository of phenomena that challenge scientific understanding and human comprehension. Among these marvels, diamagnetic levitation stands out. Known for its capacity to make objects float without the use of electromagnetism, diamagnetic materials like bismuth and pyrolytic graphite can repel magnetic fields. Suspended effortlessly above powerful magnets, these materials defy gravity, presenting an awe-inspiring spectacle that seemingly reverses the natural order of physics. The sight of a frog, side by side with water droplets, hovering serenely in space due to diamagnetic levitation captures the paradoxical tranquility and unsettling strangeness inherent in such phenomena.

Equally bewildering is the enigma of ball lightning. Ranging from golf-ball to basketball sizes, these luminous spheres have haunted the skies for centuries, often accompanying thunderstorms. The phenomenon is as unpredictable as it is mesmerizing. Eyewitness accounts document ball lightning floating peacefully across landscapes, only to explode violently, leaving scorched earth and confusion in its wake. Scientific theories attempting to dissect this optical oddity are as varied as the reported incidences themselves, yet conclusive explanations remain elusive.

Marine bioluminescence is another natural occurrence shrouded in wonder. The ability of organisms to emit light through biochemical reactions turns otherwise dark oceanic expanses into mesmerizing scenes of flickering blues and greens. This scintillating display, performed by various species—ranging from single-celled dinoflagellates to deep-sea dwellers—serves multifaceted purposes. For some, it is a survival mechanism to evade predators, while for others, it is a tool for attracting prey. In rare instances, entire waves lit by bioluminescent plankton create the illusion of glowing seas, turning the mundane into something extraordinarily ethereal.

Moving from sea to land, the occurrence of fairy rings encapsulates the strange conjunction of fungi and folklore. These naturally occurring arcs or rings of mushrooms have long been steeped in myth, often seen as portals to other realms or as sites for nocturnal dances by ethereal beings. Scientifically, fairy rings arise from the outward radial growth of fungal mycelium beneath the soil. The mushrooms themselves represent the fruiting bodies of the mycelium, forming a geometric pattern contingent on consistent environmental conditions.

Further up the atmospheric ladder, the auroras—Aurora Borealis in the northern hemisphere and Aurora Australis in the southern—offer a celestial dance of lights that borders on the otherworldly. Caused by charged particles colliding with the Earth's magnetosphere, these luminous phenomena manifest as radiant curtains of green, pink, and occasionally red. The interplay of solar winds and the Earth's magnetic field results in these visual symphonies, capable of transforming the night sky into a theater of luminescence.

On the more sinister side of nature's quirks, the mysterious hum heard in certain locales has perturbed communities worldwide. Known as the Taos Hum in New Mexico or the Bristol Hum in England, this low-frequency droning sound affects a small percentage of the population, driving them to distraction. Despite numerous scientific studies, no definitive source has been identified. Hypotheses abound, ranging from industrial machinery to atmospheric conditions, yet the hum persists in its enigmatic cadence, leaving affected individuals in a state of bewildering auditory exile.

In the realm of synesthetic phenomena, we encounter the Blood Falls of Antarctica. Scientists have discovered that this striking crimson outflow, originating from the Taylor Glacier, owes its hue to iron oxidation. Saltwater, sealed beneath the glacier for millennia, becomes rich in iron upon contact with the air, and the rust produced stains the ice with a deep, blood-like tinge. As chilling as it is fascinating, this spectacle speaks to nature's ever-surprising alchemy.

Nature's oddities extend to ephemeral beauty found in the form of Frost Flowers. These delicate, icy efflorescences form under rare conditions where moist, unfrozen ground meets freezing air temperatures. Thin layers of ice extrude from plant stems or soil, curling into fragile, petal-like structures. Their intricate formations, resembling delicate sculptural art, offer temporary glimpses into winter's artistry, vanishing as temperatures rise.

In the arid environments, the phenomenon of the Singing Sand Dunes baffles even seasoned geologists. In specific deserts, under the right conditions, sand dunes emit a resonant, humming sound when grains of sand shift en masse. This peculiar desert song, which can range from a gentle murmur to a thunderous roar, results from the synchronized movement of sand particles, creating a resonating chamber of sorts. Each dune has its unique frequency, making the melody of the sands as varied and diverse as nature itself.

These examples, each uniquely baffling, collectively highlight nature's untamed creativity. From bioluminescent seas to levitating objects, and from celestial lights to subterranean mysteries, the natural world remains a boundless source of wonder and intrigue, continually defying our understanding and reminding us of the marvels that lie just beyond the reach of our comprehension.

46: LITTLE-KNOWN SCIENTIFIC FACTS

In the tapestry of scientific endeavor, there exist numerous facts and discoveries that seldom make their way into mainstream discourse. Carl Sagan once noted that science is a way of thinking much more than it is a body of knowledge. This journey through lesser-known scientific facts aims to underscore just that—how the obscure and seemingly trivial can profoundly alter our understanding of the universe.

Imagine, for instance, the dedication it took early astronomers to chart the night sky. Largely forgotten amidst the accolades for Galileo and Copernicus was Tycho Brahe, whose detailed observational data laid the groundwork for Kepler's laws of planetary motion. Yet, Brahe's peculiar demise in 1601, reportedly from holding his bladder too long at a banquet, shrouds his scientific contributions in an air of odd trivia. Today, some suspect mercury poisoning as the true cause, adding a layer of forensic intrigue to our exploration of historical figures in science.

While Brahe used his eyes and rudimentary instruments to map the stars, modern scientists turn to particle accelerators to unveil the universe's subatomic secrets. At the Large Hadron Collider, quarks and gluons are smashed together to recreate conditions milliseconds after the Big Bang. The discovery of the Higgs boson in 2012 was not just about completing the Standard Model of particle physics; it was about confirming that the universe has a built-in mechanism for particles to acquire mass. This particle, whimsically dubbed the "God particle," encapsulates an esoteric yet fundamental aspect of our universe that remained hidden until only recently.

In the realm of astrobiology, the extremophiles—organisms thriving in conditions previously assumed to be uninhabitable—defy conventional wisdom. Their discovery in such places as deep-sea hydrothermal vents and acidic hot springs has profound implications for the search for extraterrestrial life. Tardigrades, also known as water bears, are microscopic extremophiles capable of surviving the vacuum of space, lethal radiation, and near absolute-zero temperatures. Their resilience challenges our definitions of life and prompts speculation about what other forms of life might exist on distant exoplanets.

Transitioning from the cosmic to the terrestrial, consider the phenomenon of photosynthesis. Often introduced in elementary school classrooms, its underlying complexities are staggering. The recently discovered quantum coherence in photosynthesis—the ability of plants to maximize energy efficiency by maintaining quantum states—pushes the envelope of what we know about biology and quantum mechanics. Here, the seemingly simple act of a leaf absorbing sunlight becomes an intricate dance with elements of quantum physics, underscoring nature's mastery over processes human technology struggles to replicate.

Moreover, hidden within the spectrum of human sensory perception is the overlooked sense of magnetoreception. While birds, bees, and even some mammals navigate using Earth's magnetic field, the possibility that humans might possess this capability remains contentious. A recent study suggests that certain proteins in the human retina could function as magnetoreceptors, although conclusive evidence remains elusive. If true, it might reveal an ancient, dormant sense, hinting at the untapped potential of human biology.

In a different scientific arena, the world of chemistry houses bizarre occurrences like the Mpemba effect, where hot water freezes faster than cold water. Named after Tanzanian student Erasto Mpemba, who noticed this counterintuitive phenomenon in 1963, its explanation continues to elude precise scientific consensus. Several hypotheses involving evaporation, convection, and supercooling have been proposed, but the Mpemba effect persists as a tantalizing enigma in the annals of physical chemistry.

The human brain, a storehouse of untapped cognitive mysteries, also offers up its share of surprises. The peculiar case of the "Homer Simpson gene", named for the cartoon character's famed dim-wittedness, highlights the genetic intricacies influencing intelligence. Officially designated as RGS14, it plays a role in regulating synaptic signaling and learning. In mice, absence of this gene enhances cognitive functions, suggesting potential avenues for understanding human intelligence and cognitive disorders.

Moving into the realm of temporal anomalies, the phenomenon of time dilation, predicted by Einstein's theory of relativity, is no longer mere theoretical jargon confined to physics textbooks. Verified through experiments involving precise atomic clocks placed on fast-moving planes and satellites, it demonstrates how time itself is variable and not a constant. GPS technology, which we take for granted today, must account for these relativistic effects to provide accurate positioning data. Thus, what was once an abstract concept from Einstein's thought experiments now has practical applications affecting our daily lives.

Lastly, within the depths of our oceans stir resonant mysteries of buoyancy. Counterintuitively, deep-diving mammals like sperm whales and beaked whales manage to control buoyancy through specialized lipid-filled organs known as spermaceti. By regulating the temperature of these lipids, the whales can control their buoyancy, allowing them to undertake incredible dives to prey on deep-sea squids. Such adaptations reveal not just survival strategies but also an intricate interplay between biology and physics that remains under relentless scientific scrutiny.

Each of these little-known scientific facts carries profound implications. Whether it be revealing new layers of our existence or challenging our paradigms, they serve to remind us that the boundary of our knowledge is a constantly shifting horizon. The overlooked and the obscure, far from being inconsequential, often harbor the seeds of future revolutionary insights.

47: UNUSUAL CULTURAL PRACTICES

The world is a tapestry of cultures, each thread representing a unique set of values, traditions, and rituals. This mosaic of human expression manifests in myriad practices that can seem deeply unusual to an outsider. These practices, rooted in history and often shrouded in myth, reveal the depths of human creativity and the ways in which societies adapt to their environments.

Take the Dani tribe of Papua, Indonesia, for instance. Funeral rites in this culture involve a dramatic and painful ritual. When a member of the tribe dies, the female relatives of the deceased are expected to amputate a segment of their finger as an expression of grief and mourning. The practice, known as "finger-cutting," symbolizes the pain and loss experienced by the living. It serves as an indelible mark of respect and remembrance for the departed soul. This physical act of sorrow is a compelling, if harrowing, dedication to family bonds and the cultural importance of grief.

In stark contrast, consider the lighter, albeit equally unusual custom of "La Tomatina," celebrated in Buñol, Spain. This annual event, which takes place on the last Wednesday of August, is essentially the world's largest food fight. Participants hurl overripe tomatoes at each other in a riotous display of communal revelry. The origins of this raucous tradition are somewhat murky, with several theories ranging from a local food fight among friends to a civilian protest against town councilmen. Regardless of its roots, La Tomatina has become a massive tourist attraction, drawing tens of thousands of visitors each year to partake in this messy, joyous celebration.

In another part of the globe, the Maasai people of Kenya and Tanzania engage in a dance ritual known as "Adumu" or the "jumping dance." Performed primarily by young warriors (morani), this rite of passage includes a competitive display of jumping prowess, where participants aim to leap as high as possible from a standing position. Higher jumps signify greater strength, virility, and prowess, important attributes for warriors in this semi-nomadic community. The spectacle of the Adumu, with its rhythmic chants and collective energy, is not merely an athletic contest but a profound expression of cultural values centered on bravery and physical endurance.

Meanwhile, in the Indian state of Tamil Nadu, one can witness the ancient sport of Jallikattu, conducted during the harvest festival of Pongal. Participants attempt to grab the hump of a bull and hold on while the animal attempts to escape. Jallikattu is as much a display of human strength and courage as it is a testament to the reverence for cattle in an agrarian society. Despite modern controversies and concerns over animal welfare, this practice underscores the deep, historical ties between humans and animals in many rural communities.

Travelling to Japan, the "Namahage" festival in Akita Prefecture offers an eerie yet fascinating glimpse into the cultural practices involving folklore and myth. During this New Year celebration, men dress up as demonic deities known as Namahage, donning fearsome masks and straw costumes. They visit homes to admonish children who may have been lazy or misbehaving over the past year. The Namahage's presence reinforces moral conduct, serving as a living connection to traditional beliefs in supernatural oversight and community discipline.

In Mongolia, the Naadam Festival, also known as "Eriin Gurvan Naadam" or "Three Manly Games," highlights a trio of traditional sports: wrestling, horse racing, and archery. This festival dates back to the time of the Mongol Empire and reflects the martial spirit and nomadic heritage of the Mongolian people. Each event is steeped in ritual and symbolic significance, from the elaborate garb of the wrestlers to the child jockeys racing their steeds over vast, open plains. Naadam is more than a national celebration; it is a vibrant testament to the abiding importance of physical prowess and traditional skills in Mongolian culture.

In the remote highlands of Bolivia, the Tinku Festival presents a dramatic and, to outsiders, bewildering spectacle of ritual combat. Stemming from pre-Columbian practices, the festival sees men engage in hand-to-hand fighting contests. Tinku, meaning "meeting" in the indigenous Quechua language, is an offering to Pachamama, the earth goddess. Blood spilled during these fights is believed to ensure a bountiful harvest, underscoring a form of reciprocity with the natural world that is deeply ingrained in the Andean worldview.

The "Monkey Buffet Festival" in Lopburi, Thailand, involves a banquet laid out for thousands of macaques. Fruits, vegetables, and a variety of treats are offered to these monkeys in a grand gesture of gratitude. This festival, which attracts tourists worldwide, celebrates the macaques as symbols of prosperity and good fortune. The origins of this event are believed to be tied to the Hindu epic Ramayana, in which the monkey god Hanuman plays a crucial role. Feeding the monkeys is seen as an act that ensures the blessings of these sacred creatures upon the land and its people.

In rural China, the Dong people have preserved a custom known as the "Grand Song of the Dong," or "Da Ge." This polyphonic singing tradition, performed without any musical accompaniment, is characterized by its complex harmonics and profound cultural narratives. Songs convey stories of history, love, and nature, passed down through generations. The practice of Da Ge is not merely an artistic expression but also a vital instrument for cultural transmission, unity, and collective memory within the Dong community.

These examples, scattered across diverse geographical and cultural landscapes, highlight the rich tapestries of human customs. Some practices might elicit curiosity, awe, or even discomfort, yet each offers a window into how societies navigate the complexities of existence. Through these rituals and traditions, humanity finds ways to celebrate, mourn, instruct, and connect, weaving a global tapestry of exceptionally diverse cultural expressions.

48: THE INTRICACIES OF FORGOTTEN TECHNOLOGIES

In the chronicles of human invention, some technologies sparkled brilliantly only to fade into obscurity. These forgotten technologies, though now antiquated, once embodied the peak of human ingenuity, creativity, and resourcefulness. Each held a place at the forefront of its era, shaping lives and societies before being sidelined by newer advancements. The study of these obsolete technologies not only honors the inventiveness of our predecessors but also provides a lens through which to appreciate the continuum of innovation.

Among the most fascinating of these bygone marvels is the pneumatic tube system, an intricate network of tubes and capsules used to transport small parcels and messages. As the heart of communication in many cities during the 19th and early 20th centuries, these systems were hailed as the future of urban logistics. Delicate glass roundabouts and labyrinthine subterranean pathways enabled nearly instant letter and parcel transfers between businesses and governmental departments. Despite their compelling vision of convenience, the pneumatic tubes were gradually phased out as the telephone and digital communication rendered them obsolete.

Another forgotten technology, the monowheel, once promised a singular experience in personal transportation. Invented in various forms throughout the late 19th and early 20th centuries, monowheels are vehicles that consist of a single large wheel within which the rider sits. Despite their unique design and occasional bursts of interest, practical challenges such as balance and speed control proved significant obstacles. Nonetheless, these devices were celebrated in exhibitions and experimental designs, capturing the imagination of those dreaming of futuristic travel.

In the realm of printing, the heliograph stands as a testament to the inventiveness of early communication technologies. Essentially a device for sending messages by reflecting sunlight, the heliograph was used extensively in military operations during the late 19th century. Capable of transmitting messages over long distances using Morse code, it played a pivotal role in campaigns across vast territories where conventional methods faltered. Today, with the advent of radio and satellite communications, the heliograph has been relegated to historical curiosity, though its influence persists in the annals of tactical communication.

Textile production, too, witnessed its share of forgotten technologies. The Jacquard loom, invented by Joseph Marie Jacquard in 1804, revolutionized weaving by introducing a mechanism that used punched cards to control the pattern of weaving. This precursor to modern computing technology allowed for intricate and complex designs far beyond manual weaving capabilities. While modern digital looms have replaced the Jacquard loom, its underlying principles still resonate in the context of binary programming and automation.

The railway era, marked by its robust steam locomotives, also produced a curious but short-lived innovation: the atmospheric railway. Utilizing a pipe laid along the tracks and a piston within, atmospheric railways employed atmospheric pressure to propel the train. Proposed as a cleaner alternative to steam engines, these systems saw brief periods of operation in the mid-19th century, most notably in England and Ireland. However, technical issues such as maintaining an airtight seal and practical cost-effectiveness led to their abandonment.

Early attempts at flight produced several ingenious designs that never quite took to the skies in the manner of the Wright brothers' successful airplane. One such example is the ornithopter, inspired by the flapping flight of birds. While inventors like Leonardo da Vinci sketched elaborate plans for these wing-flapping vehicles, practical concerns regarding mechanics and human strength limited their development. Though never widely operational, ornithopters embody the intense desire to emulate nature's mastery of flight.

In the medical field, trepanation stands as a bewildering example of ancient surgical practice. Involving the drilling or scraping of a hole into the human skull, this procedure was used from Neolithic times through the Renaissance to treat conditions such as head injuries or mental illness. Despite its seemingly rudimentary approach, trepanation often resulted in a surprising number of recoveries. Modern medical advancements have rendered such invasive techniques unnecessary, yet the historical persistence of trepanation offers insight into the evolving understanding of surgery and health.

The home, too, bears marks of forgotten innovations. The kitchen automation of the mid-20th century envisioned by the likes of General Motors' "Kitchen of Tomorrow" showcased devices like ultrasonic dishwashers and automated food preparation units. These elaborate prototypes aimed to herald a new era of domestic convenience, yet many of these ambitious designs never made it to general use, supplanted by simpler, more affordable household appliances that balanced innovation with practicality.

Reflecting on these forgotten technologies reveals a pattern of bold experimentation and iterative progress. Each now-obsolete invention, whether ultimately successful or not, contributed a building block in the edifice of current technological landscapes. The relics of these innovations, preserved in museums or chronicled in patents, offer a silent but profound narrative of human history and the unceasing drive toward advancement.

49: MYSTERIES OF THE HUMAN BODY

The human body, like an enigmatic novel, is full of twists, turns, and hidden secrets. We often take for granted the familiar patterns of our physiology, but beneath the surface lie peculiarities that boggle the mind. Who would imagine that the acidic environment of the stomach is potent enough to dissolve razor blades, yet we can consume an array of foods without feeling the burn? The stomach lining regenerates at an astonishing rate to keep pace with this constant corroding action, a feat that emphasizes the resilience of the human organism.

Adding to the body's list of peculiar talents is the capacity of our bones to be five times stronger than steel, pound for pound. While this might sound like the stuff of legends, the reinforcing qualities of this biological material often go unnoticed until a fracture occurs. The temporary transformation of stem cells into osteoblasts—the cells responsible for new bone formation—demonstrates the body's remarkable ability to heal itself, a mechanism finely tuned over millennia of evolution.

Oddities do not end with our robust skeletal framework. Consider the phenomenon of hyperthymesia, a condition where individuals possess an extraordinary autobiographical memory. These rare few can recall minute details from almost every day of their lives, offering a panoramic view of their personal history that most can only dream of. While a boon in many ways, it is not without its burdens, as the inability to forget even trivial moments can become overwhelming.

Skin, the body's largest organ, houses its own share of peculiar wonders. Capable of regenerating entirely every month, it serves as our first line of defense against the outside world. An even more astonishing fact is the sheer quantity of microorganisms that call our skin home—colonies of bacteria numbering in the millions. These microscopic organisms form a complex ecosystem, balancing between guarding against pathogens and contributing to skin health. A fascinating if somewhat disconcerting relationship, highlighting the body's intricate alliances with other forms of life.

Our sensory organs, too, are repositories of curiosities. The human tongue boasts a topographic map of taste buds uniquely sensitive to five primary flavors: sweet, salty, sour, bitter, and umami. Interestingly, there's evidence suggesting that the perception of a flavor can be influenced by multiple senses; what we see, hear, and even smell can enhance or diminish taste. The variability and adaptability of sensory perception showcase an ability to evolve according to environmental contexts, tailoring experience in subtly complex ways.

The heart, often romanticized as the seat of emotion, functions with mechanical accuracy, maintaining life through its rhythmic contractions. Intriguingly, it continues to beat in synchronized cadence even when detached from the body, so long as it receives adequate oxygen supply. This resilience is due to a specialized group of cells known as pacemaker cells that autonomously regulate the heartbeat. It's a relentless engine, symbolizing both the fragility and fortitude of human existence.

Exploring internal anomalies, we encounter the mysterious world of the human microbiome. Our intestines are home to trillions of microorganisms that aid in digesting food, synthesizing vitamins, and regulating immune responses. This microbial population is so vital that alterations in its composition are linked to various health conditions, from depression to inflammatory diseases. The symbiotic relationship between these microbes and their human host raises compelling questions about the interconnectedness of life within and around us.

Advancing to cellular dynamics, telomeres play an essential role in the aging process. These protective caps at the ends of chromosomes shorten with each cell division, often considered a biological clock counting down to cellular senescence. Emerging studies suggest that lifestyle factors such as diet, exercise, and stress management can influence the length and integrity of telomeres, implicating them as key players in the narrative of aging and longevity.

In the catalog of anatomical anomalies, the wonders of the human eye stand out. Able to distinguish over a million shades of color, our eyes are unparalleled in sensitivity and speed. The retina, a thin layer of tissue at the back of the eye, processes visual information with an efficiency surpassing even the most advanced cameras. Despite its complexity, the eye can adapt to an extensive range of lighting conditions, automatically adjusting to the nuances of our environment.

Finally, consider the paradoxical phenomenon of phantom limb syndrome, where amputees experience sensations, often painful, in limbs that are no longer present. Neural pathways in the brain seem to retain a map of the missing limb, triggering sensations that defy the mere physical absence. This enigma of neural plasticity provides a glimpse into the profound, sometimes baffling ways in which human consciousness interprets bodily existence.

50: ODDITIES IN ART AND LITERATURE

Navigating the realm of art and literature reveals a tapestry of unusual forms and expressions that challenge conventional aesthetics. Imagine, for example, the art of Giuseppe Arcimboldo, an Italian painter whose 16th-century works comprised intricate portraits made entirely from fruits, vegetables, flowers, and other natural objects. Arcimboldo's compositions, such as "The Summer" and "The Winter," are visually striking and subversive, forcing the viewer to reconsider everyday objects in new and imaginative ways. His bizarre style foreshadowed surrealism, advocating for a fluid boundary between reality and fantasy long before Salvador Dalí popularized the genre.

Meanwhile, the world of literature has no shortage of oddities. Consider the Oulipo (Ouvroir de Littérature Potentielle), a group of French-speaking writers and mathematicians founded in 1960 who created constrained writing techniques. Georges Perec, one of its most renowned members, authored "La Disparition," a 300-page novel entirely devoid of the letter "e." This lipogrammatic tour de force, translated into English as "A Void," demonstrates the creative potentials of limitations. The story is secondary to the structure itself, serving as an exercise in linguistic dexterity and demonstrating how constraints can lead to extraordinary creative output.

In the realm of visual arts, Outsider Art or Art Brut showcases works created outside the boundaries of official culture. These artists, often self-taught and operating on the fringes of society, produce raw and unfiltered expressions of their inner worlds. Henry Darger, a reclusive custodian from Chicago, is celebrated for his monumental work, "The Story of the Vivian Girls," a 15,000-page epic accompanied by hundreds of multi-colored illustrations. Darger's intricate and fantastical worlds, populated by heroic children and grotesque monsters, invite viewers into a deeply personal and unsettling universe that defies mainstream artistic standards.

Performance art also offers a platform for the unconventional. Viennese Actionism, a radical and controversial art movement from the 1960s, pushed the boundaries of physical and psychological endurance. Leading figures like Hermann Nitsch and Günter Brus utilized their bodies as canvases, subjecting themselves to extreme acts involving self-inflicted pain, nudity, and ritualistic dismemberment of animal carcasses. These performances, intended to confront and unsettle, sought to express raw human emotions and societal critiques in ways traditional art forms could not.

Turning to literary genres, the world of Bizarro Fiction stands out for its dedication to the unconventional. With roots in speculative and absurdist literature, this genre embraces the weird, the grotesque, and the fantastical in equal measure. Titles like Carlton Mellick III's "Satan Burger" and Jeremy Robert Johnson's "Skullcrack City" invite readers into worlds where logic is suspended and the narrative boundaries are elastic. These works revel in their strangeness, offering an outlet for readers weary of formulaic storytelling.

Consider further the creations of Mark Z. Danielewski, whose novel "House of Leaves" embodies literary experimentation. The book's unconventional narrative structure—where text spirals, overlaps, and disorients as much as it narrates—immerses readers in a labyrinthine experience mirroring the story's haunted house. Footnotes weave multiple tales within the central plot, altering traditional reader engagement and challenging linear conceptions of novelistic form.

Historical context often enriches the story behind odd artistic and literary endeavors. In the early 20th century, the Dada movement emerged as a response to the horrors of World War I. Emphasizing absurdity, anti-art, and spontaneity, Dadaists like Marcel Duchamp disrupted traditional art. Duchamp's "Fountain," a porcelain urinal signed "R. Mutt," redefined art's boundaries and provoked essential questions about authorship, originality, and the nature of artistic expression that continue to resonate.

Surrealism also offered fertile ground for the strange and the unexpected. Leonora Carrington's visual and literary works meld surrealist fantasy with deeply personal symbolism. Her paintings and writings often derived from her fascination with alchemy, mythology, and the occult, depicting fantastical creatures and dreamlike landscapes that blur reality's edges. Carrington's unique voice enriched the surrealist movement, emphasizing the power of the unconscious in artistic creation.

Finally, Gothic literature's eerie atmospheres and supernatural elements have left an indelible mark on the literary landscape. Horace Walpole's "The Castle of Otranto," considered the first Gothic novel, blends medievalism, horror, and romance. Walpole's tale, featuring haunted castles and ancestral curses, laid the groundwork for subsequent Gothic masterpieces like Mary Shelley's "Frankenstein" and Bram Stoker's "Dracula," continuously drawing readers into their dark, fantastical realms.

Art and literature's oddities serve as testaments to human creativity's boundless potential. Each piece, whether a surreal portrait, a labyrinthine novel, or an extreme performance, expands our understanding of what art and literature can be, inviting us to explore the edges of our imagination.

51: OUTLANDISH LEGAL CASES

In the small town of Salem, Alabama, in 1887, a courtroom drama unfolded that would become a testament to the quirks of American jurisprudence. The case involved a farmer named Amos Adams who was sued by his neighbor, Leonard Hopkins, over a rooster accused of "disturbing the peace." Hopkins claimed that the incessant crowing of Adams' rooster at the break of dawn caused him severe mental distress and disrupted his sleep. The judge, in an attempt to maintain order and fairness, summoned the rooster to the courtroom. The bird, predictably, crowed, much to the amusement and chagrin of the court attendees. Astonishingly, the judge ruled in favor of Hopkins, ordering Adams to either silence the rooster or face recurring fines. This case, while ostensibly trivial, sheds light on the idiosyncrasies of rural law and the extents to which legal systems must adapt to unique complaints.

In the realm of criminal law, outlandish cases often overlap with the bizarre and unsettling. In 2005, Robert Lee Brock, an inmate at the Indian Creek Correctional Center in Virginia, made headlines by filing a $5 million lawsuit against himself, claiming that he had violated his own civil rights by getting arrested. Brock's argument was built on the premise that his self-inflicted crimes resulted in his incarceration, which deprived him of his freedom and created a financial burden. His audacious plea for the state to pay the settlement since he was without income drew both ridicule and a degree of sympathy for its ingenuity. Unsurprisingly, the court dismissed his self-filed lawsuit, leading to discussions about the mental state and desperate ingenuity of inmates.

The case of United States vs. One Book Called Ulysses is another landmark that highlights the peculiar interplay between literature and legality. James Joyce's novel "Ulysses," published in 1922, faced widespread bans due to its explicit content. In 1933, Random House, the American publisher, sought legal endorsement to publish the book in the United States. The trial was held in the Southern District of New York before Judge John M. Woolsey. After scrutinizing the novel's content, Woolsey delivered an unprecedented verdict, acknowledging the book's artistic value and ruling that it was not obscene. His ruling paved the way for greater freedom in literary expression and set significant precedents for future obscenity cases.

Another notable and jaw-dropping legal case occurred in 1995 in the field of tort law. Known as the "McDonald's coffee case," Stella Liebeck sued the fast-food chain after suffering third-degree burns from spilled hot coffee purchased at a drive-thru window. The media portrayal often simplified the narrative, failing to capture the severity of Liebeck's injuries and the underlying claims. However, during the trial, it was revealed that McDonald's served coffee at a temperature hotter than many other restaurants, and the company had faced numerous previous complaints. The jury awarded Liebeck $2.7 million in punitive damages, later reduced by the judge. This case highlighted corporate negligence and consumer safety, igniting extensive debates about tort reform and the balance between personal responsibility and corporate accountability.

In a display of legislative absurdity, the "Monkey Selfie" case of 2011 traversed the boundaries of intellectual property law. Photographer David Slater set up equipment in the Indonesian jungle, which was then used, albeit inadvertently, by a macaque named Naruto to take a series of selfies. These images went viral, leading to a heated legal battle over the ownership of the photographs. PETA filed a lawsuit on behalf of Naruto, arguing that the monkey should be considered the owner and entitled to the profits. The case was pivotal in questioning the definition of legal personhood and the assignment of intellectual property rights to non-human entities. Ultimately, the Ninth Circuit Court of Appeals ruled that animals do not have standing to claim copyright under the law, yet the discussion it spurred about the rights of animals and their potential claims in a legal context remains poignant and unresolved.

One of the most ludicrous yet officially recorded cases in British legal history dates back to 1310, aptly named the "Trial of the Pyx." In this bewildering event, a pig was put on trial for allegedly striking and killing a child. The trial, complete with witnesses and legal representation for the pig, followed the full formality of judicial proceedings customary for human defendants. This anthropomorphizing of animals in legal contexts, though archaic, showcased how societal interpretations of justice and accountability were applied rigorously, even to animals incapable of understanding or participating in the legal process. Although such trials are inconceivable today, they serve as a bizarre reminder of how legal systems evolve and reflect the cultural understanding of justice.

From roosters in rural America to macaques in Indonesian jungles, and from prison cells to literary liberation, these outlandish legal cases demonstrate the elasticity and, at times, the eccentricity of the judicial system. They reveal the legal community's ongoing struggle to balance the letter of the law with the unpredictable peculiarities of human—and sometimes animal—behavior.

52: THE WONDERS OF CRYPTIDS AND MYTHICAL CREATURES

The world of cryptids and mythical creatures is a realm that intersects between folklore, occasional witness testimonies, and the slim fragments of evidence that persistently keep legends alive. These creatures captivate the human imagination, filling the gaps of our understanding with wondrous, and sometimes eerie, possibilities. From the dense forests of North America to the remote highlands of Scotland, tales of enigmatic beings have been part of human culture for millennia.

A classic example is Bigfoot, also known as Sasquatch. This elusive creature is said to dwell in the dense forests of the Pacific Northwest. Descriptions of Bigfoot depict it as a large, bipedal, ape-like being covered in hair. Sightings date back many years, supported by fuzzy photographs and ambiguous footprints. Despite extensive searches and numerous expeditions, conclusive evidence remains elusive. Yet, the persistence of the legend speaks volumes about human fascination with the unknown and hidden aspects of our world.

Another captivating cryptid is the Loch Ness Monster, affectionately known as Nessie. Originating from the chilly waters of Loch Ness in Scotland, Nessie has been described as having a long neck and a humpback, reminiscent of ancient plesiosaurs. The modern legend of Nessie began in the early 20th century, bolstered by countless sightings and underwater sonar explorations that captured inexplicable blips. Skeptics attribute these sightings to misidentifications of mundane objects or animals, yet the myth endures, drawing tourists from around the world.

Venturing into the folklore of the African continent, we encounter the Mokele-Mbembe. Reported to inhabit the Congo Basin, this creature is often described as a large, sauropod-like entity. Some local tribes regard it with fear and reverence, while Western explorers and cryptozoologists have mounted expeditions in search of this elusive beast. While no definitive proof has been captured, the legend persists, driven by the intrepid spirit of discovery and the allure of uncharted wilderness.

In the heart of Latin America, tales of Chupacabra strike a chord of both curiosity and fear. Translating to "goat-sucker," Chupacabra stories emerged in the 1990s and typically describe a creature that preys on livestock, leaving behind drained bodies. Eyewitnesses report sightings of a reptilian-like or alien-like beast, while skeptics argue these accounts are the result of hysteria or misidentifications of ordinary animals suffering from disease. Yet, the myth continues to evolve, melding with cultural narratives and the human penchant for mystery.

Dragons, widespread in the myths and legends of numerous cultures, capture the essence of awe-inspiring yet fearsome creatures. Eastern dragons, particularly in Chinese mythology, are often depicted as benevolent, wise, and powerful beings associated with water and rain. They are revered as symbols of strength and good fortune. In contrast, Western dragons tend to embody chaos and destruction, often guarding treasures or serving as antagonists in heroic tales. These contrasting depictions highlight the cultural variations in ascribing meaning and values to mythical creatures.

The Yeti, or the Abominable Snowman, occupies the high altitudes of the Himalayan mountains. Descriptions portray it as a large, ape-like creature adapted to icy terrains. Sherpa communities have woven the Yeti into their spiritual and cultural fabric, speaking of its presence with reverence. Western explorers and mountaineers have also contributed to the legend through sporadic sightings and mysterious footprints. The harshness of the environment adds to the scarcity of evidence, leaving the Yeti's existence shrouded in a tantalizing blend of possibility and skepticism.

In the realm of maritime folklore, mermaids and sirens beckon with their captivating yet dangerous allure. These aquatic beings, depicted as half-human and half-fish, are entrenched in the lore of sailors across cultures. Some tales speak of their beauty and enchanting songs, capable of luring sailors to their doom. Others portray mermaids as benevolent entities guiding ships to safety. With origins in Greek mythology, these beings encapsulate the human fascination with the sea's mystery and the dual nature of beauty and peril.

These stories and creatures persist not merely out of idle fancy but because they tap into a fundamental human impulse – the desire to explore, to push the boundaries of the known, and to find meaning in the unexplained. Whether nestled in secluded corners of the globe or dwelling in the depths of our collective psyche, these enigmatic beings continue to ignite curiosity, invite skepticism, and inspire countless adventures into the realms of the unknown.

53: QUIRKY ARCHITECTURAL MARVELS

In the northwestern expanse of Spain stands the Cathedral of Justo, a decades-long labor of love built mostly by a single man, Justo Gallego Martinez. Without formal architectural training or official building permits, Justo used salvaged materials to construct this edifice that rivals many professional designs. He began his work in 1961, using whatever resources he could scrounge—old bricks, broken tiles, donated materials—to erect walls soaring high with windows that cast vibrant mosaics onto the dusty floor below. Though incomplete for much of his life, the cathedral exemplified human ingenuity and unyielding spirit.

Thousands of miles away, another testament to idiosyncratic architecture rises from the dry Arizona desert: Arcosanti. This experimental town, envisioned by Italian architect Paolo Soleri, blends architecture and ecology into an ambitious concept known as "arcology." Begun in 1970, Soleri envisioned a self-sustaining community minimizing environmental impact. Designed to house 5,000 people, Arcosanti's actual population has remained much smaller, tending to hover around 80 residents. Featuring apse-like structures and vaults, the town merges organically with the arid landscape, presenting an ongoing experiment in alternative living.

Across the Atlantic and into France lies the Palais Idéal, a castle borne from the dreams of Ferdinand Cheval, a postman with a penchant for the fantastic. This stone structure, visually akin to something plucked from the mind of a fairy tale author, emerged gradually as Cheval meticulously collected stones on his daily mail route. Building with his hands alone, he spent 33 years assembling an eclectic blend of motifs—Hindu temples, Egyptian ruins, medieval forts—crafted painstakingly into one fluid, surrealistic structure. Cheval's commitment to his vision earned the project recognition from artists and architects alike.

A simpler yet still bizarre architectural wonder exists in the Czech Republic: Prague's Dancing House. Designed by Frank Gehry and Vlado Milunić, this building curves and sways like a pair of dancers. Known locally as Fred and Ginger, a nod to the famous dance duo Fred Astaire and Ginger Rogers, the building's non-linear aesthetics stand out sharply amid the Baroque and Gothic facades that typify Prague. Completed in 1996, it exemplifies deconstructivist architecture, challenging conventional notions of form and structure with its fluid, dynamic design.

In Japan, the Nakagin Capsule Tower in Tokyo represents another curious chapter in architecture. Completed in 1972 by Kisho Kurokawa, the tower epitomizes Metabolism, an architectural movement merging timelessness of traditional vernacular with the forward-looking design of machines. The building features 140 prefabricated capsule units, bolted individually to a central shaft. Each pod, designed as a minimalist, self-contained living space, is starkly utilitarian, with a single round window standing out against the small, stark interiors.

Meanwhile, the southern reaches of India house a monumental tribute to disbelief: the Matrimandir in Auroville. This golden domed structure, described as a "place for individual silent concentration," emerged from a utopian idea envisioned by The Mother, a counterpart to the famous Indian philosopher Sri Aurobindo. The spherical structure, underpinned by four major pillars representing elements necessary for the collective consciousness, exudes an aura of serenity and meditation. Encapsulated within a sprawling garden, Matrimandir's design does not adhere to any traditional religious or cultural symbols, making it an ethereal outlier among devotional architectures.

Nestled in the Scottish countryside, Rosslyn Chapel exudes an air of mystique amplified by its esoteric carvings and serpentine legends. Founded in 1446 by William Sinclair, 1st Earl of Caithness, the chapel is replete with stone carvings depicting symbols that some speculate to connect with the Knights Templar or the Holy Grail. Intricate carvings, from angels playing bagpipes to the infamous Apprentice Pillar, enrich the walls with celestial and terrestrial iconography, inviting speculation and theories, none conclusively proven, enhancing its enigmatic allure.

In Berlin, the design of the Hundertwasserhaus defies modernist sensibilities with its vibrant, organic forms and rainbow hues. Austrian artist Friedensreich Hundertwasser believed that architecture should be an extension of nature, characterized by amorphous lines and ecological harmony. Completed in 1985, the apartment complex appears as a living organism, replete with undulating floors, irregular windows, and rooftop vegetation blending seamlessly with the surrounding greenery, all hallmarks of Hundertwasser's philosophy that beauty requires irregularity and color.

Each of these structures presents not just a divergence from architectural norms, but a manifestation of human eccentricity and creativity. Their existence is a testament to the limitless potential of human imagination, showing that bricks and mortar can be molded into unprecedented forms, and that architecture, at its core, is as much about the dreams and quirks of its creators as it is about providing shelter and utility.

54: THE WORLD OF UNCOMMON PHOBIAS

Phobias, those irrational and persistent fears, lurk in the back of human consciousness, often manifesting in peculiar and surprising ways. While common phobias like arachnophobia (fear of spiders) or claustrophobia (fear of confined spaces) are well-known, there exists a subset of phobias that challenge our understanding of fear itself due to their rarity and sheer oddness.

Take, for instance, anatidaephobia—the fear that somewhere, somehow, a duck is watching you. This phobia stems not from an aggressive encounter with a duck but from an overwhelming and inexplicable anxiety about being observed by a duck. Those living with anatidaephobia might avoid parks or rural areas where ducks are likely to be found, not because they fear an attack, but because they fear the unsettling notion of being surveilled by waterfowl.

Another uncommon phobia, somniphobia, is the fear of sleep. Unlike insomnia, which is an inability to sleep, somniphobia encapsulates the dread of falling asleep. This fear can derive from various psychological origins, such as the fear of losing control, dread of nightmares, or even a phobia of dying in sleep. Those suffering from somniphobia might go to great lengths to stay awake, leading to severe physical and mental health consequences due to chronic sleep deprivation.

Ablutophobia presents another curious case—the fear of bathing or washing. Individuals with ablutophobia may have undergone traumatic childhood experiences involving baths or showers, leading to an ingrained fear of cleanliness. This can result in social stigmatization, as well as health issues due to poor hygiene. The avoidance of washing can become a significant impediment in daily life, affecting quality of life and social interactions.

Trypophobia is not classified as a typical phobia, but it incites aversion or fear through clusters of small holes or bumps. While it might sound obscure, images of things like honeycombs, lotus seed pods, or even aerated chocolate can trigger intense discomfort or disgust in those affected. Current theories suggest that this reaction may be rooted in an innate unease triggered by certain visual patterns associated with disease or danger.

Imagine living with omphalophobia, the fear of belly buttons. This phobia can encompass both an aversion to one's own navel and a compulsion to avoid seeing or touching other people's navels. The origins of omphalophobia are likely multifaceted, stemming from cultural taboos, personal traumatic experiences, or even the symbolic significance of the belly button as a reminder of human vulnerability and birth.

Xanthophobia, the fear of the color yellow, seems especially bewildering. One might ponder how a color can elicit such fear. However, this phobia can be severe, where individuals may avoid anything yellow, including common objects like flowers, clothing, and even foods. The pathology behind xanthophobia can be traced to negative associations or traumatic events that involved the color yellow, creating a complex psychological response of aversion or panic upon encountering this hue.

Pogonophobia, the fear of beards, can create societal challenges in cultures where facial hair is prevalent or even revered. Those with pogonophobia may experience unease or repulsion at the sight of beards, affecting their interpersonal relationships and potentially limiting their social interactions to clean-shaven individuals. The causes of pogonophobia might trace back to negative encounters with bearded individuals or cultural influences where beards are portrayed negatively.

Similarly perplexing is chorophobia, the irrational fear of dancing. Individuals who suffer from chorophobia might avoid social gatherings or environments where dancing occurs, stemming from a fear of dancing themselves or witnessing others dance. The roots of this fear can relate to anxiety over public embarrassment, cultural prohibitions, or traumatic experiences related to dance.

The fear of long words, known as hippopotomonstrosesquipedaliophobia, presents a paradox in its very name. It highlights the irony and sometimes the absurdity that accompanies certain phobias. This phobia can cause significant anxiety in educational or literary contexts, limiting a person's willingness to read, write, or communicate where long or complex words are involved.

Phobias, common or rare, insignificant or debilitating, offer a window into the human psyche, revealing how deeply personal experiences, cultural influences, and biological predispositions intertwine to create fear. The world of uncommon phobias serves as a cognitive echo chamber where seemingly trivial or abstract stimuli can provoke profound psychological responses. Understanding these uncommon phobias not only expands our knowledge of human fear but also encourages empathy for those who navigate life under the shadow of these irrational yet very real fears.

55: ANOMALIES IN SPACE EXPLORATION

In the vast expanse of space, anomalies aren't just the exception; they're often the norm. Space exploration, with its precise calculations and stringent protocols, sometimes encounters the completely unexpected—events, phenomena, and machinery that defy explanation and seem plucked from science fiction.

When NASA launched the Pioneer 10 spacecraft in 1972, it was expected to journey to Jupiter and then continue on a path out of the solar system. What the engineers and scientists hadn't anticipated were the enigmatic readings they received years later. Pioneer Anomaly, as it became known, was a mysterious deviation in the spacecraft's trajectory. Despite extensive calculations and reviews, the slight but undeniable deceleration puzzled experts. The anomaly led to numerous hypotheses, from mundane explanations involving heat emission to the more exotic suggestions of new physics. It remains one of the tantalizing puzzles of interstellar travel.

Space missions often require ingenuity, leading to some quite peculiar designs and missions. The Soviet Union's Lunokhod 1, an uncrewed lunar rover, was conceived in the 1960s and launched in 1970. Unlike other rovers, it had a rather unorthodox road test—trundling around the streets of a city near the factory where it was built. Engineers navigated it through city traffic, simulating the remote operations they would later conduct from Earth. The sight of a tank-like contraption maneuvering through urban landscapes drew considerable curiosity and serves as a reminder of the creative lengths to which space scientists sometimes go.

In 1984, astronaut Bruce McCandless II drifted further away from the confines of his spacecraft than any other human in history. Using the Manned Maneuvering Unit (MMU), essentially a nitrogen-propelled jetpack, he floated freely in space, untethered. This image, an astronaut against the backdrop of infinite black, embodies the vast and uncharted territory of space. However, the MMU was retired not long after due to concerns over its safety and the inherent risks associated with being so far from a return path. This brief episode showed both the boldness and caution of human space endeavors.

Cosmic anomalies are not limited to human-made objects. Space itself is a tapestry of peculiar events. Consider the phenomenon of Fast Radio Bursts (FRBs). These are incredibly short, ultra-strong pulses of radio waves originating billions of light-years away. Discovered only in the last decade, FRBs defy comprehensive explanation. Some speculate they might be from the remnants of exploding stars, while others entertain the far-fetched theory of alien civilizations. The search for their origin continues, representing the deep-seated human desire to comprehend the universe's enigmatic signals.

Nature's anomalies also force us to rethink our technological paradigms. In 1962, the Alouette 1, a Canadian satellite used to study the ionosphere, made a bizarre discovery. It found what appeared to be a "whistling" noise—a product of electromagnetic waves traversing the Earth's magnetosphere. The phenomenon, known as Whistler Waves, had been predicted but never observed so clearly before. Alouette 1's surprising find paved the way for extensive research into space weather and electromagnetic interactions, influencing spacecraft design and communication.

Even the most routine missions have their unexpected moments. In 1972, Apollo 16, a mission intended chiefly for lunar exploration, stumbled upon a mystery while in orbit around the Moon. The crew captured a series of photographs showing what appeared to be unidentified objects tracking the spacecraft. Dubbed the "Apollo 16 UFO Incident," various explanations surfaced over the decades, from reflections off the spacecraft window to distant debris. Despite official debunking, curiosity about the incident persists, fueling theories and debates among space enthusiasts.

Space debris itself is a substantial anomaly. On the one hand, it's a byproduct of our increasing presence in orbit—defunct satellites, spent rocket stages, and fragments from disintegration or collisions. On the other hand, the sheer scale of this collection of unnatural artifacts is staggering. The 2009 collision between the defunct Russian satellite Kosmos-2251 and the operational Iridium 33 highlighted the issue starkly, leading to thousands of new debris pieces that continue to orbit Earth. Managing and mitigating space debris has become critical, prompting innovative solutions like harpoons, nets, and even robotic janitors designed to clean up our cosmic clutter.

Another fascinating anomaly involves the behavior of liquids in space. Without the influence of gravity, fluids form perfect spheres due to surface tension. This can complicate drinking, as demonstrated by astronauts in microgravity using a simple straw and a carefully calibrated beverage containment system to quench their thirst. More importantly, these fluid dynamics impact essential systems like fuel tanks and life-support mechanisms, necessitating a detailed understanding of how liquids behave in the space environment.

The quest for understanding space has also led to the development of unique astronaut gear, often designed with seemingly odd purposes in mind. Extravehicular Mobility Units (EMUs), the suits designed for spacewalks, must endure temperature extremes from -250°F to 250°F. To counteract this, modern spacesuits are equipped with Liquid Cooling and Ventilation Garments (LCVGs), garments embedded with a network of thin tubes circulating water to stabilize body temperature. Even the simplest actions—like staying cool—require intricate systems when performed in space.

Yet, among these anomalies and curiosities, space exploration continuously propels humanity forward—each anomaly, a puzzle piece in the larger cosmic picture.

56: THE CULTURE OF CONSPIRACY THEORIES

Conspiracy theories have been part of the human experience for centuries, infusing history with intrigue, suspicion, and often, elaborate tales that straddle the line between fiction and reality. They find their roots in the human tendency to seek patterns and understand the unknown through connecting disparate dots. This chapter delves into some of the most outlandish conspiracy theories, revealing their origins and how they have perpetuated through time.

One of the most enduring conspiracy theories is the notion that the moon landing was a hoax. This theory gained traction shortly after the first moon landing in 1969 when NASA's Apollo 11 mission successfully transported Neil Armstrong and Buzz Aldrin to the lunar surface. Detractors pointed to the fluttering American flag (despite the lack of atmosphere), the unusual lighting in photographs, and supposed inaccuracies in the astronauts' shadows. Despite the overwhelming scientific evidence and testimonies from astronauts, this theory persists, fueled by skepticism of government narratives and a misunderstanding of space photography principles.

Another compelling conspiracy theory involves the assassination of President John F. Kennedy in 1963. Officially, Lee Harvey Oswald was the lone gunman responsible for the tragic event. However, the theory that there was a second shooter, more often referred to as the "grassy knoll theory," has maintained a strong presence in public consciousness. Numerous books, documentaries, and even Oliver Stone's film "JFK" have explored possible connections to organized crime, the CIA, and other government entities. This theory reflects the discomfort people feel with seemingly simple explanations for such earth-shattering events.

The Roswell UFO incident of 1947 is another staple of conspiracy lore. When an unidentified flying object crashed near Roswell, New Mexico, the military initially claimed it was a weather balloon. However, witnesses reported seeing metallic debris and non-human remains, sparking rumors of a government cover-up. This event gave rise to Area 51, the secretive military base supposedly housing extraterrestrial technology and life forms. This theory touches on humanity's fascination with outer space and the possibility of life beyond our planet.

Conspiracy theories also extend to global organizations. The Bilderberg Group, an annual private conference of influential people in business, finance, media, and politics, is often the center of conspiracy theories alleging a secret plan for world domination. Critics suggest that the conference is a forum for shaping global policies out of public scrutiny. While the secrecy and exclusivity of the meetings create fertile ground for speculation, most evidence points to less nefarious purposes, such as networking and discussing global issues.

Social and psychological factors often drive the propagation of conspiracy theories. Cognitive biases, such as confirmation bias, play a significant role. People tend to favor information that confirms their preconceptions, which makes it easy for conspiracy theories to gain a foothold. The internet has exponentially amplified this effect, creating echo chambers where conspiracy theories can thrive unchecked by factual verification.

The anti-vaccination movement epitomizes how conspiracy theories can have substantial real-world consequences. The discredited study by Andrew Wakefield in 1998 falsely linked the MMR vaccine to autism, a claim that has been thoroughly debunked by subsequent research. Nevertheless, the idea took hold and has led to decreased vaccination rates and outbreaks of preventable diseases. This highlights the danger of conspiracy theories when they intersect with public health.

The tragic events of September 11, 2001, spawned numerous conspiracy theories as well. Known as the "9/11 Truth Movement," proponents argue that the attacks were either orchestrated or allowed to happen by elements within the U.S. government to justify subsequent military actions. They point to perceived anomalies in the collapse of the World Trade Center buildings and discrepancies in official reports. Despite comprehensive investigations and debunking efforts, these theories continue to find adherents.

The Flat Earth theory, perhaps one of the most visually striking conspiracy theories, posits that the Earth is flat rather than spherical. Despite overwhelming evidence to the contrary, including satellite images and the physical appearance of the Earth from space, some claim that a massive cover-up involves scientists, astronauts, and governments. This theory thrives particularly in an era of increasing mistrust of experts and institutions.

The common thread across these diverse conspiracy theories is the intrinsic human desire to make sense of disorder and uncertainty. When faced with monumental or inexplicable events, many people gravitate toward elaborate narratives that offer clear villains and motives. Conspiracy theories can serve as coping mechanisms, providing a sense of control and understanding in a seemingly chaotic world.

57: UNFAMILIAR FACTS ABOUT FOOD AND DRINK

Many common foods and beverages possess histories and attributes that rarely cross the minds of those who consume them daily. The simple act of enjoying a cup of coffee, for example, connects individuals to a web of history and culture that stretches across continents and centuries. Coffee's journey begins in the ancient coffee forests of Ethiopia. Legend has it that a goat herder named Kaldi discovered the beans after noticing his animals becoming particularly energetic after eating the berries. These beans eventually found their way to the Arabian Peninsula, fostering the spread of coffeehouses, which served as centers for the exchange of information much like today's internet cafes.

Consider the potato, a staple in diets around the world. Native to the Andean region of South America, the potato was first domesticated by the Incas over 7,000 years ago. When the Spanish conquistadors encountered these tubers, they initially dismissed them as unimportant. However, the potato's journey to Europe in the 16th century marked the beginning of a substantial agricultural transformation. Despite initial suspicion and even accusations of causing leprosy, the potato eventually gained acceptance. Its nutritional value and ability to grow in diverse climates rendered it a crucial crop, significantly impacting European societies by staving off famine and contributing to population growth.

The history of chocolate also reveals unexpected twists. Originating from the seeds of the cacao tree, chocolate was consumed by pre-Columbian cultures like the Aztecs and Mayans as a bitter beverage mixed with spices. Only after the Spanish conquest of the Americas did the transformation of chocolate from a sacred ceremonial drink to a sweet confection begin. Spaniards added sugar and cinnamon to this concoction, thereby altering its form and paving the way for its introduction to European nobility. Chocolate's evolution from an exotic indulgence to a ubiquitous treat underscores the power of cultural exchange and adaptation.

Exploring the spice trade uncovers another layer of global interconnectedness. Spices like black pepper, cinnamon, and nutmeg not only served culinary purposes but also played pivotal roles in the economic and political histories of societies. In medieval Europe, spices symbolized wealth and status, making them highly coveted commodities. The quest for these aromatic treasures fueled maritime exploration, leading to historic voyages such as those by Vasco da Gama. The discovery of sea routes to the spice-rich lands of Asia irrevocably changed the world's economic landscape.

The humble carrot, now often associated with health and nutrition, was not always the bright orange vegetable known today. Originally, carrots came in a variety of colors, including purple, yellow, and white. It wasn't until the 17th century, during the Dutch Golden Age, that orange carrots were cultivated to honor the House of Orange, the Dutch royal family. This development aligns with broader trends in selective breeding that have shaped agricultural practices.

In the realm of beverages, the history of beer offers a glimpse into ancient civilizations. Beer is one of the oldest prepared beverages, with evidence suggesting its production dates back to 5,000 BCE in what is now Iran. Early beer was far different from the bottled versions seen today, known as "liquid bread" for its thick, nutritious quality. Sumerian tablets feature the hymn to Ninkasi, the goddess of brewing, which doubles as both a praise and a recipe, illustrating how integral beer was to daily life. Over time, brewing techniques evolved, incorporating hops in place of other bittering agents and refining the fermentation process, leading to the diverse global beer culture enjoyed today.

Cheese, another ancient food, possesses origins as serendipitous as they are practical. Legend attributes its discovery to an Arab trader who stored milk in a container made from a sheep's stomach, only to find it curdled into a tangy, solid mass by the end of his journey. Different cultures have since developed countless varieties, each reflecting local tastes, climates, and resources. Regions like the French Roquefort caves or the Italian Swiss Alps have given rise to distinctive flavors that capture their environments, with certain cheeses becoming protected as cultural and culinary heritage under international law.

Even the seemingly mundane apple carries stories that reach back to antiquity and mythology. The domesticated apple, Malus domestica, originated in the mountains of Kazakhstan. From there, the apple spread westward via the Silk Road and through the migrations of traders and conquerors. The ancient Greeks and Romans cultivated numerous varieties, each suited to different purposes, from eating fresh to brewing cider. Apples also became embedded in folklore and mythology, such as the tale of the golden apples of the Hesperides in Greek mythology and the story of Isaac Newton and the theory of gravity.

Teasing apart the layers of everyday edibles exposes a rich tapestry woven from countless threads of human ingenuity, cross-cultural exchanges, and historical circumstance. The paths these foods and drinks have travelled to become ingrained in contemporary diets reveal much more than culinary habits; they tell of migrations, trade, and transformation that have influenced civilizations over millennia.

58: UNCOMMON SPORTING EVENTS

In a small town in Finland, thousands gather each year to witness a spectacle peculiar to that region—the Wife Carrying World Championship. Originating from the 19th-century era of "Ronkainen the Robber," spectators are treated to various forms of man efficiently carrying their wives through an obstacle course with water hazards and sand traps. The event, far from a mere display of brute strength, showcases remarkable ingenuity and agility. The peculiar race rules stipulate that the wife being carried must be at least 49 kilograms. If she falls below this weight, she is required to wear a backpack to make up the difference. The winning couple receives the wife's weight in beer.

Meanwhile, in the United States, the Redneck Games hosted in Georgia stand out as a satirical take on the Olympic Games. Participants engage in mud pit belly flops, seed spitting, and hubcap hurling. Conceived in the mid-1990s as a tongue-in-cheek response to the Atlanta Olympics, this event gained its unique charm through its unabashed embrace of Southern stereotypes. Each year a throng gathers to witness the extraordinary competencies of contestants willing to leap into mud pits or launch hubcaps with impressive accuracy.

Across the globe, Southern Italy offers the town of Ivrea's Battle of the Oranges. This historical reenactment dates back to the 12th century and symbolizes the townsfolk's rebellion against a tyrannical lord. Participants divide into two teams and pelt each other with oranges in a high-energy, citrus-flavored enactment of their historic revolt. Oranges from Sicilian groves arrive in truckloads to ensure ample ammunition. Despite the occasional bruise, the spirited event is a testament to Ivrea's fierce dedication to its historical lore.

Australia boasts its own unique competition—the annual Cockroach Races in Brisbane. Celebrated since 1982 as part of the Australia Day festivities, these races take place at the Story Bridge Hotel, where dozens of cockroaches vie for victory in specially constructed racing tracks. Entrants can bring their own 'roach or rent one from the host establishment. Coursing through the designated paths, these insects fuel a quirky form of excitement among the attendees, who cheer as if watching thoroughbred horses.

In a cozy Japanese village, the Crying Sumo Competition turns wrestling conventions on their head. Held in Tokyo, this unusual contest involves pairs of Sumotori holding crying babies. The champion is the one who can make the infant cry the loudest in the shortest time frame. Shinto priests oversee the ritualistic event, which has its roots in ancient beliefs that a baby's tears can ward off evil spirits and promote healthy growth. This curious liaison between tradition and sport captures the very essence of human cultural complexity.

The Scottish Highlands are home to the ancient tradition of the Caber Toss, a mainstay of the Highland Games. Men in kilts attempt to flip large, wooden poles end over end. These cabers, reaching up to 6 meters in length and weighing over 70 kilograms, must be flipped to land in a straight line for maximum points. This demanding test of strength and precision has been a fixture of Scottish heritage for centuries, drawing participants from around the globe to prove their mettle.

Certain northern climates hold the peculiar sport of reindeer racing, particularly vibrant in regions of Norway and Finland. This contest involves contestants skiing behind galloping reindeer, tethered by reins. The spectacle, a crossover between cross-country skiing and traditional animal racing, is embedded deeply in the local Sami culture. For many, it's more than sport; it's an affirmation of cultural identity and a celebration of subsistence practices that have endured for generations.

Japan also boasts the All-Japan Kanamara Penis Festival, an event flush with folklore and wrapped in a spectacle of color and revelry. Central to the festivities is a parade featuring enormous phallic shrines carried through the streets, a ritual believed to help protect against diseases and promote fertility. While not a sporting competition in the traditional sense, the event's exuberant parades, ceremonial contests, and frenzied communal participation mark it as a unique cultural sport.

In Gloucestershire, England, the Cooper's Hill Cheese-Rolling and Wake draws spectators and participants who unabashedly fling themselves downhill in pursuit of a rolling round of double Gloucester cheese. Braving steep declines and uneven terrain, competitors often tumble headlong in their attempts to catch the cheese, which accelerates to speeds touching 70 miles per hour. Despite injuries, this age-old practice, believed to date back centuries, endures as a symbol of unchecked zeal and community festivity.

In Thailand, the yearly Monkey Buffet Festival is an odd yet endearing spectacle where tables laden with fruits, vegetables, candies, and soft drinks are set for the local monkey population. Human participants and the hordes of macaques share in this outlandishly entertaining dining experience, capturing the symbiotic relationship between the humans and animals of Lopburi. Far from an athletic contest, it encapsulates the remarkable breadth of what constitutes a festival in different parts of the world.

From Finnish wife carrying to Thai monkey buffets and Australian cockroach derbies, uncommon sporting events celebrate the bizarre, the traditional, and the downright eccentric. They offer windows into the local cultures and histories that birthed them, standing as vibrant testaments to human creativity, community spirit, and the sheer joy of the unconventional.

59: THE QUIRKINESS OF TIMEKEEPING

The history of timekeeping is a fascinating tale of human ingenuity and our relentless pursuit of precision, marked by quirks and eccentricities that reflect the diversity of human cultures. As human civilization evolved, the need for more precise timekeeping became evident. Early humans likely used simple methods to mark the passage of time, perhaps noticing the cyclic patterns of the sun and moon. Ancient civilizations gazed at the heavens, navigating the celestial bodies to measure days, months, and years. As societies grew more complex, so too did their methods of measuring time.

One of the earliest and most iconic timekeeping devices is the sundial, developed by the Egyptians around 3500 BCE. The principle behind the sundial is remarkably simple: a gnomon, or a shadow-casting rod, is positioned in such a way that as the sun moves across the sky, the shadow it casts moves around a marked surface, indicating the time of day. This remarkably intuitive tool laid the foundation for more sophisticated timekeeping methods, though sundials were obviously useless at night or during cloudy weather, highlighting their inherent limitations.

Around the same time, other civilizations were developing unique approaches to timekeeping. The Babylonians, with their penchant for astronomy and mathematics, contributed significantly to our understanding of time. They used a base-60 number system, which is why we still divide an hour into 60 minutes and a minute into 60 seconds. Their timekeeping system blends practicality with a mystical reverence for numerical systems, demonstrating how intertwined culture and mathematics can be.

In ancient China, early water clocks, or clepsydrae, introduced the idea of measuring time by the steady flow of water. These clocks allowed water to drip into a container at a constant rate, with marks on the container indicating the hour. While ingenious, these devices were limited by their susceptibility to temperature changes and other environmental factors. Despite these challenges, water clocks were used for centuries, continuously refined by various cultures. Ancient China also developed incense clocks, where different scents marked the passage of time, illustrating the diversity in human approaches to the concept of time.

As we fast forward to the Middle Ages, mechanical clocks began to surface, largely in European monasteries. These early mechanical clocks relied on complex systems of gears and weights to keep time. Monks used them to signal times for prayer, embedding timekeeping deeply into religious practices. The incorporation of an escapement mechanism, a crucial innovation, regulated the release of energy to advance the gears at a consistent rate, leading to more accurate time measurement. One such example is the clock in the Salisbury Cathedral, built around 1386, one of the oldest surviving mechanical clocks in the world.

The pursuit of accuracy in timekeeping continued into the Renaissance, culminating in the invention of the pendulum clock by Christiaan Huygens in 1656. Pendulum clocks were much more accurate than their predecessors, deviating by only a few seconds per day. This breakthrough enabled the development of accurate maritime navigation. John Harrison's marine chronometer, created in the 18th century, solved the problem of determining longitude at sea, a dilemma that had plagued sailors and explorers for centuries. Harrison's chronometers drastically reduced the dangers of long maritime journeys and facilitated global trade networks and the expansion of empires.

The 20th century saw another leap forward with the introduction of quartz clocks. Quartz clocks, introduced in the 1920s, utilize the piezoelectric properties of quartz crystals, making them incredibly accurate and reliable. These clocks democratized precise timekeeping, making it accessible to the masses. By the mid-20th century, timekeeping had reached new pinnacles with the development of atomic clocks. These devices measure time by tracking the vibrations of cesium or rubidium atoms, achieving unparalleled precision. Atomic clocks are so accurate that they can measure time with an error margin of about one second every million years. This degree of precision is essential for modern technologies like GPS, telecommunications, and even the synchronization of power grids.

Yet, even in the era of atomic clocks, humanity's fascination with unconventional timekeeping persists. The Doomsday Clock, introduced in 1947 by the Bulletin of the Atomic Scientists, symbolizes the perceived likelihood of global catastrophe, particularly nuclear war. Its hands have oscillated over the decades, reflecting the world's fluctuating geopolitical tensions, illustrating the convergence of timekeeping and sociopolitical commentary.

Among the most quirky modern timekeeping devices is the Moscow Time Clock, installed in 1999 at the All-Russian Exhibition Center. This clock doesn't just tell the time; it displays the current phase of the moon, the position of the planets, and the calendar date according to the ancient Slavic calendar. This blend of modern and archaic elements epitomizes the rich, multifaceted nature of humanity's relationship with time. Similarly, the Long Now Foundation's 10,000 Year Clock project, designed to tick once a year with a century hand that advances every 100 years, reorients our perspective from the immediate to the epochal, advocating for a stewardship that transcends individual lifespans.

Timekeeping, as a discipline, is as diverse and layered as the cultures and societies that have contributed to its evolution. From sundials and water clocks to atomic precision and symbolic doomsday clocks, our methods of measuring time reflect not just our technological advances, but also our philosophical musings. Through the lens of time, we glimpse the depth of human ingenuity and the profound desire to anchor ourselves within the vast expanse of the cosmos, ever striving to understand and control the passage of time.

60: THOUGHTS ON RANDOMNESS

Randomness is a concept that permeates many aspects of life, influencing everything from the behavior of particles at the quantum level to the unpredictability of human decisions. It is a force that operates in the background of existence, shaping events in ways that are often beyond our comprehension. Despite its apparent lack of structure, randomness is a subject that has intrigued mathematicians, scientists, and philosophers for centuries, leading to the development of theories and ideas that seek to explain its nature and role in the universe.

At its core, randomness refers to the occurrence of events that lack any predictable pattern or sequence. In mathematics, randomness is often associated with probability theory, which provides a framework for measuring the likelihood of different outcomes. The study of probability dates back to the 17th century, when mathematicians such as Blaise Pascal and Pierre de Fermat began exploring the mathematics of gambling and games of chance. Their work laid the foundation for modern probability theory, which remains a crucial tool for understanding randomness.

One of the central ideas in probability theory is that of the random variable. A random variable is a numerical representation of the outcome of a random event, such as the roll of a die or the flip of a coin. These outcomes are assigned probabilities that reflect their likelihood of occurring. For example, in the case of a fair six-sided die, each of the six possible outcomes—1, 2, 3, 4, 5, and 6—has an equal probability of 1/6. This concept of assigning probabilities to different outcomes is fundamental to the study of randomness and allows for the quantification of uncertainty.

Probability theory also introduces the concept of expected value, which represents the average outcome of a random event over many trials. In the case of a fair six-sided die, the expected value of a roll is 3.5, even though this value is not one of the possible outcomes. This seemingly paradoxical result highlights the abstract nature of mathematical expectations, as they represent an average that emerges over a large number of iterations rather than an individual occurrence. Variance, another key concept in probability, measures the spread of outcomes around the expected value, providing insight into the degree of randomness present in a given system.

Randomness plays a significant role in the natural world, where it manifests in a variety of forms. One of the earliest documented observations of randomness in nature is Brownian motion, the erratic movement of small particles suspended in a fluid, first described by the botanist Robert Brown in the early 19th century. This phenomenon results from the constant bombardment of the particles by molecules in the surrounding fluid, causing them to move in unpredictable directions. Brownian motion is a classic example of randomness at work in the physical world, and its study laid the groundwork for the development of statistical mechanics and the kinetic theory of gases.

On a smaller scale, randomness is a fundamental feature of quantum mechanics, the branch of physics that deals with the behavior of subatomic particles. In the quantum realm, particles do not have definite positions or velocities until they are measured, and their behavior is governed by probabilities rather than certainties. The Heisenberg Uncertainty Principle, a cornerstone of quantum theory, states that it is impossible to know both the position and momentum of a particle with perfect accuracy. This inherent uncertainty leads to randomness in the behavior of quantum systems, where outcomes can only be described in terms of probability distributions. The exact moment when a radioactive atom will decay, for example, is fundamentally unpredictable and can only be expressed as a probability over a given time period.

In biology, randomness plays a crucial role in the process of evolution. Genetic mutations, which are random changes in the DNA sequence of an organism, provide the raw material for natural selection to act upon. Some mutations may confer a survival advantage, while others may be neutral or even harmful. Over time, these random variations accumulate, leading to the diversity of life we see today. While the process of natural selection is deterministic in its favoring of beneficial traits, the randomness of mutation and environmental changes introduces an element of unpredictability into the evolutionary process.

Beyond the natural sciences, randomness has a profound impact on human behavior and decision-making. In the field of psychology, the concept of random reinforcement is used to explain why certain behaviors are more persistent than others. Random reinforcement occurs when rewards are given intermittently and unpredictably, rather than at fixed intervals. This type of reinforcement is known to be particularly effective in shaping behavior, as it creates a sense of uncertainty that encourages individuals to continue engaging in the rewarded activity in the hope of receiving the next reward. This principle is widely used in the design of gambling games, where the unpredictable nature of winnings keeps players coming back despite repeated losses. Similarly, the random nature of social media notifications and video game rewards taps into this psychological mechanism, fostering addictive behavior.

Human beings also tend to exhibit a bias known as apophenia, the tendency to perceive patterns or connections in random or meaningless data. This cognitive bias leads people to find meaning in randomness, seeing patterns where none exist. Apophenia is responsible for phenomena such as seeing shapes in clouds, hearing hidden messages in music played backward, and interpreting coincidences as significant events. This inclination to impose order on chaos reflects our deep-seated desire to make sense of the world, even when faced with randomness.

The philosophical implications of randomness are far-reaching and have been the subject of debate for centuries. One of the central questions is whether true randomness exists, or whether what we perceive as random is simply the result of incomplete knowledge. This debate often centers around the ideas of determinism and indeterminism. Determinists argue that every event has a cause, and that if we had complete knowledge of all variables, we could predict every outcome with certainty. From this perspective, randomness is an illusion created by our ignorance of the underlying causes. Indeterminists, on the other hand, contend that some events are fundamentally random and cannot be predicted, even with perfect knowledge. The advent of quantum mechanics has lent support to the indeterminist view, as it suggests that randomness is an intrinsic feature of the universe at the smallest scales.

Another philosophical question raised by randomness concerns its relationship with free will. If our actions are determined by prior causes, as determinists suggest, then do we truly have the freedom to choose our paths? Alternatively, if our actions are influenced by random factors beyond our control, does that undermine the notion of free will? These questions challenge our understanding of human agency and responsibility, blurring the line between chance and choice.

Randomness also plays a vital role in fields such as cryptography and computer science, where it is used to ensure security and unpredictability in digital systems. Cryptography relies on random numbers to generate secure keys that protect sensitive information from unauthorized access. The strength of cryptographic systems depends on the quality of the randomness used to generate these keys. As a result, researchers have developed sophisticated methods for generating truly random numbers, such as measuring the decay of radioactive particles or capturing environmental noise.

In the realm of simulations and modeling, randomness is harnessed through techniques such as Monte Carlo simulations. These simulations use random sampling to model complex systems and make predictions about the likelihood of different outcomes. Monte Carlo simulations are widely used in fields such as finance, engineering, and physics, where they allow researchers to estimate probabilities and optimize decision-making in uncertain environments. By incorporating randomness into their models, scientists and engineers can better understand the behavior of systems that are too complex to predict with complete certainty.

Despite its seemingly chaotic nature, randomness is not synonymous with disorder. In many cases, random processes give rise to structures and patterns that exhibit a high degree of organization. This phenomenon is observed in fields such as statistical physics, where the collective behavior of large numbers of particles, each moving randomly, can produce ordered patterns such as crystal lattices or phase transitions. Similarly, in biology, the random mutation of genes leads to the emergence of complex organisms that are highly adapted to their environments.

AFTERWORD

Thank you for taking the time to wander through the labyrinth of curiosities in *Random Knowledge Volume One*. This book was a labor of love, crafted for those who delight in the unexpected and find beauty in the seemingly trivial. As you've discovered, the world is full of strange, fascinating, and often overlooked details that enrich our understanding of life and the universe, even if only for the sake of sheer wonder.

Throughout these pages, we've explored topics that range from the bizarre to the profound. Some of the knowledge presented may have sparked new interests or made you see familiar things in a different light. Perhaps you now view urban animals with a new sense of respect, or maybe you've developed a curiosity about the mechanics of cat purring or the secrets buried within time capsules. The purpose of this collection was never to answer life's biggest questions, but rather to invite you into a space where the obscure meets the ordinary in unexpected ways.

In writing this book, I wanted to create a space where readers could revel in the small moments of discovery, where facts didn't have to be practical to be valued. This collection is a reminder that knowledge comes in many forms, and sometimes the most delightful insights are the ones that don't fit neatly into the categories of "useful" or "necessary." They are simply interesting for their own sake, adding texture to the fabric of our understanding.

As you close this book, I hope you walk away with a renewed sense of curiosity. Perhaps the next time you encounter an odd historical figure, an unexplained natural phenomenon, or an obscure cultural tradition, you'll find yourself diving deeper into its story, eager to uncover the randomness that shapes our world. If nothing else, I hope this volume has reminded you of the joy in learning something new, no matter how small or unusual.

This is just the first volume in what I hope will be a long journey through the odd and wonderful corners of knowledge. Stay curious, keep asking questions, and never underestimate the power of a seemingly useless fact to brighten your day or spark your imagination. Until the next volume, thank you for joining me on this adventure through the peculiar and the profound.

May your curiosity never be satisfied.

— Bing Dingo

ACKNOWLEDGEMENT

I want to acknowledge the countless sources of inspiration that contributed to *Random Knowledge Volume One*. From the many books, articles, and documentaries that provided the seeds for these chapters, to the conversations with friends, family, and fellow trivia enthusiasts that sparked new ideas, this book is the result of a wide web of influences. Thank you to the many researchers, historians, scientists, and storytellers whose work makes this kind of exploration possible.

To my family and friends, thank you for tolerating my endless enthusiasm for obscure facts and for supporting me through the long process of writing and editing this book. Your patience, encouragement, and humor have been invaluable, and I could not have completed this project without you.

I also want to acknowledge the independent authors and creators who inspire me daily. The world of independent publishing is a vibrant and challenging space, and I am grateful to be a part of a community that values creativity, curiosity, and the pursuit of unconventional ideas.

Lastly, a special thank you to the reader who will inevitably come across a random fact in this book and use it to win a trivia night, impress a friend, or simply brighten their day. You are the reason I write, and I hope this book brings as much joy to your life as it brought to mine in creating it.

— Bing Dingo

Printed in Great Britain
by Amazon